Jennifer Trainer Thompson

THE fresh EGG COOKBOOK

FROM CHICKEN TO KITCHEN
Recipes for Using Eggs from
Farmers' Markets, Local Farms,
and Your Own Backyard

Storey Publishing

The mission of Storey Publishing is to serve our customers by
publishing practical information that encourages
personal independence in harmony with the environment.

Edited by Margaret Sutherland and Sarah Guare
Art direction by Mary Winkelman Velgos
Book design and text production by Amanda Jane Jones

Cover photography by © Jason Houston (back) and © Mars Vilaubi (front and spine)
Interior photography by © Jason Houston, except for © Adam Mastoon: pages 10 (top and
    bottom) and 11 (fourth from top); © Debbi Smirnoff/iStockphoto.com: page 10 (second
    from top); © Edd Westmacott/Alamy: page 11 (bottom); © Jennifer Trainer Thompson:
    pages 3 and 59; © Mars Vilaubi: pages 10 (third from top) and 11 (fifth from top); Mars
    Vilaubi: pages 15, 101, and 109; and © National Geographic Image Collection/Alamy:
    page 11 (top three)
Photo styling by Catrine Kelty
Food preparation by Jody Fijal

Indexed by Christine R. Lindemer, Boston Road Communications

Storey Publishing
210 MASS MoCA Way
North Adams, MA 01247
www.storey.com

Printed in China by Toppan Leefung Printing Ltd.
10 9 8 7 6 5

Library of Congress Cataloging-in-Publication Data

Thompson, Jennifer Trainer.
  The fresh egg cookbook / Jennifer Trainer Thompson.
     p. cm.
  Includes index.
  ISBN 978-1-60342-978-8 (pbk. : alk. paper)
  1. Cooking (Eggs) 2. Cookbooks. 3. Chickens—Breeding.
  4. Eggs—Production. I. Title.
TX745.T46 2012
641.6'75—dc23
                        2011025028

"A good fresh tribute to good fresh eggs."

Roy Blount Jr.

"Made with a true egg, even the friendliest fried-egg-over-easy is once again sublime. And now that people are starting to experience the difference between the real thing and the pallid supermarket version, it's a good time to revisit all those wonderful egg dishes (and some new ones) that may have been forgotten but are worth reviving. Personally, I can't wait to make Jennifer's popovers!"

Deborah Madison, author of *Local Flavors: Cooking and Eating from America's Farmers' Markets* and *Vegetarian Cooking for Everyone*

"This is a lovely and eminently practical book to have handy on your kitchen shelf — chock-full of sensible and delicious ways to put fresh eggs to good use. But beware: Once you've tasted a fresh egg, there's no going back. If you've ever even considered keeping your own chickens, *The Fresh Egg Cookbook* just might be the catalyst for buying the coop!"

Danny Meyer, coauthor of *The Union Square Cafe Cookbook*

"Sculptural, earthy, and oh-so-versatile, fresh eggs have captured the imagination of Jennifer Trainer Thompson, who has written a timely and entertaining egg-centric cookbook. She offers practical information about raising chickens (easy!), and her mouthwatering recipes range from the simple (classic egg salad sandwich) to the sublime (soufflé glacé au citron)."

Vicky Lowry, Executive Editor of *ELLE DECOR*

"A delightful introduction to the pleasures of backyard chickens, *The Fresh Egg Cookbook* is filled with helpful information for those who want to start their own flock and great-looking recipes for those who already have."

Elizabeth Kolbert, author of *Field Notes from a Catastrophe: Man, Nature, and Climate Change*

DEDICATION

While it may take a coop, not a village, to keep chickens, it also takes sustained effort on my family's part, and I dedicate this book to Isabel and Trainer, as well as Big Joe Daddy-O . . . not to mention the late Hot Wheels, who helped us set it all in motion.

ACKNOWLEDGMENTS

I'd like to thank those who shared recipes with me, including Jeanne Besser, Verna Thompson, Judith Thompson, Mary Jane Thompson, Cecilia Hirsch, Darra Goldstein, Doug Carver, and my husband, Joe. I'd also like to extend special kudos to Jody Fijal, my loyal recipe tester; stylist Catrine Kelty; photographer Jason Houston; and Cathy Dow, who babysits all my chicks with humor and aplomb. What a great team! I am also thankful to those who shared their chicken tales: John Gerry, Laura Schoenbaum, and Lauren Gotlieb. We love our gals.

I'm also so pleased to be in bed with, or at the very least, cooped up with, the folks at Storey Publishing, who are housed in the nineteenth-century mill campus of MASS MoCA along the Hoosac River, which flows past my house. I can bike to meet my editor for coffee, and am grateful to Pam Art, Margaret Sutherland, Sarah Guare, Mary Velgos, Deborah Balmuth, Dan Reynolds, Alee Marsh, and Amy Greeman at Storey for welcoming me under the Workman umbrella.

INTRODUCTION

"Omne vivum ex ovo."
(All life comes from an egg.)
— Latin proverb

Nine years ago, my father suggested that I walk over to his neigh-bors' yard with my four-year-old son, Trainer, to see their chickens.

Chickens?

My father lived near Boston, in a cul-de-sac of trim Cape Cod houses, paved driveways, and manicured rhododendrons . . . not particularly rural by any stretch. Curious, we went over. Their flock of feathered hens was taking in the warm spring afternoon, pecking, clucking, eyeing us quizzically with heads cocked, and making jerky movements that were full of nervous personality. We were amused. I peppered the neighbor with the usual questions: How did he build a coop in the back of his garage? What do they eat? How does he protect the chickens from predators? He reached under a sitting hen in her nest (she gave a disgruntled squawk) and pulled out a few brown speckled eggs for us to take home. As I tucked them into my jacket pocket, I noticed they were still warm. I kept touching them, fondling them, really, relishing the feel and shape all the way home. I left them in a basket on the kitchen counter until morning.

The next day I scrambled them with milk and a few snips of chives, and dished them up with toast, bacon, and coffee. They were great. And hard to crack! What hit me first was the yolks' color — a deep, gorgeous orangey yellow, like a New York City taxicab or wild French marigolds. The yolk membrane was stronger than I was used to, making the yolks seem plumper. The whites were thicker, too, resisting the race to the outer edges of the skillet when cracked. What cinched the deal was the taste; I'd always thought an egg is an egg is an egg, but this was richer than I could imagine, the nuanced result of a natural diet of grasses, clover, bugs, and grub worms. Little did I know that this little oval also held a perfect nutritional profile: An egg is an excellent source of protein, second only to mother's milk, with all 9 essential amino acids and 13 essential vitamins, mostly in the yolk, which is also one of the few foods that naturally contain vitamin D. Plus, it's low in fat, with only 5 grams per egg.

Driving home to the Berkshires at the end of the weekend, I silently contemplated having chickens for about a minute, then ruled it out as a crazy idea. After all, I had a busy life, with a husband, a career, and a four-year-old. I never mentioned it to my husband, Joe. Then a few months later, out of the blue, he suggested the idea of raising chickens. A family project? In which we share the pleasures of the table and shoveling the coop? I was in.

STARTING FROM SCRATCH

We knew zilch about raising chickens when we began. We'd oohed and aahed over prized heirloom breeds at the annual Martha's Vineyard agricultural fair. While we were vacationing in Puerto Rico, our neighbors' hens would often hop the fence and scratch around our yard, once leaving a little brown calling card of an egg in Joe's sandal in the bathroom. Living in the country, we'd always embraced a can-do philosophy, from shoveling snow off the porch roof to digging a smoke pit in our backyard (Joe even lined the two earthen chambers with stones dug from the pit — they don't call our hill Pine Cobble for nothing). So converting a little shed in our yard into a coop one weekend wasn't a big deal.

Soon we were experiencing the winter pleasures of catalogs arriving from the Murray McMurray Hatchery in Texas. On cold winter nights, we'd fuss over the cute chick photos. By springtime, we were checking out not only the sugar shacks that come alive on Vermont's Route 7 corridor when the sap starts flowing but also the feed stores

along the way, looking for baby chicks and heat lamps. By Easter, we just jumped in and did it. Without a peep.

THE CHICKEN CRAZE

We weren't the only ones diving into a chicken-raising adventure. Chickens are now something of a fad, with a cult following that borders on obsession: a poultry show in Germany two years ago attracted more than 70,000 chickens and their owners; in New Haven, Connecticut, where zoning codes have ruled fowl illegal since the 1950s, town officials introduced legislation to allow residents to raise up to six hens each; and the Charlottesville League of Urban Chicken Keepers has formed CLUCK, a network of backyard poultry enthusiasts dedicated to raising chickens in Virginia. Call it a chicken coup, but even renowned designers from Martha Stewart to Bunny Williams are rearing feathered friends in luxurious backyard quarters, deriving inspiration from these operatic personalities. "The mix of stripes, polka dots, and fringe on some chickens looks like the ensembles you see on the runways of the French haute couture," writes Dan Shaw, whose lively blog Rural Intelligence keeps a pulse on what's happening in northwestern Connecticut and the Berkshires.

There are even hens in the 'hood. When a rooster fell off the back of a truck in Brooklyn a few years back, hardened New Yorkers acted like a village and raised him. They crowed to the press that they loved the sound of the alarm clock as he made a home in Prospect Park. They brought him their food scraps and water on hot days. They named him Light Bulb. Someone even brought him a pair of hens. Indeed, all across the country, cities are revising their ordinances to accommodate the micro–chicken farming movement, as people keep them cooped up everywhere from suburban mudrooms to urban co-ops.

What's not to love about them? There are many benefits to raising chickens. It's fun and deeply satisfying to homestead on a minor level and experience the joys of country living with heirloom birds, though be forewarned: It's a slippery slope from there to keeping bees, tapping maple trees, and shearing your own sheep. At a time when so many people crave a closer connection to nature, there's something incredibly sweet about waking up and finding fresh eggs waiting for you. I love eating the eggs from animals that we trust, take care of, and nurture.

I also love coming home and seeing our ten "girls" pecking through the grass, sometimes roaming the yard, always expressing themselves. *New Yorker* writer Betsy Kolbert told me she sometimes pulls up a chair to the fence simply to watch her hens. I agree; how can you not be mesmerized by a bird that is a dead ringer for Carol Channing? In the summer, when we have parties that spill into the yard and musicians break out their instruments, the girls come up to the fence and stare at us like statues, listening raptly to the music. There's also a thrill to finding a nest of eggs ranging in color from blue to white to brown. Collected in a wicker basket, they make a far better house gift than wine or flowers.

Especially if you have children, chickens make excellent pets; they are independent, low maintenance (unlike a dog, they can take you or leave you), and surprisingly affectionate, with comical personalities that make you laugh, a quality that should not be underestimated. Quite social, they flock together in the barnyard by day and huddle together on a perch at night. Once, when a raccoon climbed down a tree near our coop and stole one of our hens, I knew the minute I came home that evening that something was wrong because her barnyard buddy was squawking mournfully, keening almost, alerting us and the world that something was dreadfully wrong. And when all's right with the world, they let me know that too, flapping down the drive when the school bus announces Trainer and his sister Isabel's return home, or waddling across the yard to greet me . . . though, if truth be told, it's usually when they see a pot of apple peels or other scraps in my hand.

Besides, how can you not love a hen dubbed a Polish Frizzle?

GET CRACKING

Over the years, as I've watched our kids interact with the hens, I'm struck by the fact that they have a natural sense of where some of their food comes from, if not which came first. When I was a kid, we'd eat a lot of hard-boiled eggs in the summer — on our boat on weekends, at the beach, at family parties — but it never occurred to me to connect the dots to the food source. They came from the refrigerator. Nor did it seem out of the ordinary (it wasn't in those days) when my mother and I went to the A&P in the winter and the only lettuce in the cooler was iceberg.

By the time I was in my early 20s and living in New York, thanks to Frieda's and Flying Foods, you could get mahimahi in the city in January, or grouper in Indiana in December, or kiwifruits anywhere, anytime. I remember hearing Alice Waters speak at a conference in the mid-'80s, lambasting people for the fact that they weren't eating more locally, and though I appreciated her sentiment, I also found myself thinking that this gal had obviously never lived in the Northeast Kingdom, where one can go five months without seeing the ground. Now the locavore trend has gained enormous momentum, and urbanites and suburbanites have their own hens and cows. At the end of the day, I'm grateful that it's completely natural for my kids to pick the Brussels sprouts and green beans that they eat in the summer, and to collect the eggs that their hens lay year-round.

We've been raising hens for almost a decade, and I love it. I feel more in tune with the source of my food and even nature. Eating from my own backyard never tasted so good. Just last weekend we had waffles made with our own eggs for breakfast, accompanied by our own maple syrup and butter that my daughter, Isabel, had made in Brownies. It was heavenly.

According to legend, the number of folded pleats in a chef's toque once represented the number of ways he could cook an egg, Any chef in sixteenth-century France worth his salt could cook an egg at least 100 ways, and formal chefs still wear hats with 100 starched pleats. I've included more than 100 recipes and ideas here, and encourage you to sit back, have fun with the idea . . . and get cracking.

Why Fresh Is Best

There's a discernible difference between eggs from hens given free range in a pasture and supermarket eggs from hens raised in a processing plant. The first is often age: a supermarket egg may be a month or even two months old, whereas you know the freshness of your hens' eggs. The fresher the egg, the richer the flavor. Fresh eggs are also a little bit more difficult to work with when both poaching and peeling, as the egg white is less malleable.

There's also often a difference in the yolk's color, which is influenced by diet: a yard bird that forages for bugs and greens and is fed food scraps will produce a deeper yellow, almost orange yolk (see egg below) than that of a hen raised in a processing plant (see egg at top). (Someone from Louisiana said that when she feeds her hens scraps from a crawfish boil, the yolks are bloody orange.) Those deep yellow yolks also taste richer, a result of both their freshness and the hen's diet.

There are also differences in nutritional content. According to a 2007 *Mother Earth News* study, eggs from hens raised in a pasture may be substantially more nutritious than supermarket eggs. They contain up to six times more vitamin D, two times more omega-3 fatty acids, more vitamins A and E, and up to one-third less cholesterol. What's not to love about fresh eggs?

Everything You Might Want to Know

(but were too embarrassed to ask)

I must confess that when starting down the chicken path, I was out of touch with my inner hen and ignorant about some chicken basics . . . like whether you need a rooster for a hen to lay an egg. (You don't.) For those who want to talk turkey, here are some interesting facts.

- An egg's color is determined by the layer's breed, not by what the hen ate. Brown, blue, and white eggs all taste the same. Interestingly, most hens with white earlobes lay white eggs and those with red earlobes lay brown eggs.

- Hens (females) lay eggs. Roosters (males) do not. Both are chickens. *Pullets* are female chickens less than a year old.

- You don't need a rooster for a hen to lay an egg. And no matter how long a hen sits on an egg, it will not turn into a chick unless the egg has been fertilized by a rooster. Think of a woman's reproductive system: The eggs travel from a woman's ovaries monthly, but they need sperm to be fertilized.

- Once in a blue moon, a hen will lay a double-yolked egg (think identical twins).

- Depending on the breed, a hen will lay 200 to 300 eggs a year, but she never lays more than one egg a day.

- Chickens like to sleep standing up.

- Hens have no teeth — hence, "scarce as hen's teeth." Food is swallowed whole, stored and softened, then digested in the gizzard, which is in the bird's stomach. People give their chickens grit (pebbles) to help with the processing.

- Hens start laying eggs at 4 to 6 months, although they sometimes won't lay if the weather's below freezing or above 90°F (32°C). Their fertility peaks at 2 years, then falls off quickly. Most hens, if not picked off by predators, will live for 8 to 15 years.

- Fertilized eggs, if not fully incubated by the hen, are edible. The eggs need a mother hen sitting on them for about 21 days in order to hatch.

My Top 10 Breeds

With more than 200 breeds of chickens, which is right for you? That depends on what you're looking for — eggs? meat? temperament? laying ability? hardiness in cold weather? My top-ten list reflects that I am a fan of heirloom varieties.

Araucana (blue and green eggs). Also known as the South American Rumpless, this bird has no butt or tail. Calm, friendly birds that look a little rumpled (unlike the stately Buff Orpingtons), Araucanas can be hard to find at hatcheries but are worth the quest — their blue and green eggs are conversation starters. They seem to know they've got something special: they are not the most productive hens in the world, favoring charm over output.

Australorp (brown eggs). Developed in Australia in the early 1900s from Black Orpingtons, this bird caused a sensation in the '20s when one hen laid 364 eggs in one year, long before the intensive-light techniques used in hatcheries. They've never come close to such fertility since, but are still great layers and a popular heritage breed due to their hardy disposition, docile personality, and handsome appearance.

Buff Orpington (brown eggs). Originally developed in Orpington, England, in the 1880s, this sweet, beautiful bird is big and fluffy with a lovely temperament. They are average layers, but their beauty makes up for that.

Dominique (light brown eggs). Developed in New England in the early 1800s, this breed had a rough go of it; according to the *Book of Poultry*, published in 1910, it was in danger of sinking into oblivion, a victim of the "money making breeds of American fowl." It held on, however, and recently there has been a revived interest in this heirloom breed. Good mothers who can endure rugged weather, these birds are quiet and docile.

Leghorn (white eggs). An ancient bird that was honored by the Romans and is popular today worldwide, the Leghorn can be noisy, even flighty, and excitable, but also friendly; it'll be the first from the flock to greet you when you come home. Leghorns are prolific layers, making them the favored breed for mass production. Although pooh-poohed by some, give them a break. They are dependable, and after all, you need white eggs to dye at Easter.

• •

New Hampshire Red (brown eggs). New Hampshire's answer to the Rhode Island Red, this is a handsome bird with a rich chestnut coat, a curious disposition, and prodigious laying abilities.

• •

Plymouth Rock (light to medium brown eggs). This large, cold-hardy bird with its distinct zebra pattern tends to be tame, dependable, and long lived, making it perfect for a backyard flock. Developed in New England in the mid-1800s, the Plymouth Rock breed has seven varieties, including the Barred Rock.

• •

Polish (white eggs). This breed can be high maintenance, and it isn't the hardiest bird due to its fancy plumage, but it is tame and a good layer, and provides comic relief with its puffball crest.

• •

Rhode Island Red (brown eggs). The star of the barnyard, this is the mahogany red bird you see in New England folklore illustrations of the nineteenth century. It tends to be quiet and docile, is robust in harsh weather, and is a dependable, productive layer. Originally bred in Little Compton, Rhode Island, these birds can be aggressive with other chickens or if provoked (this is especially true of roosters), although if raised with love, they can become quite loving and attached to you.

• •

Sussex (creamy white to light brown eggs). Developed in Sussex, England, in the early 1800s, these kind-tempered birds are alert yet docile, making them great children's pets. Pretty and fluffy, they are good layers and popular backyard chickens in many countries.

WHICH CAME FIRST?

Classics

"The egg can be your best friend if you just give it the right break."
— Julia Child

Once we made the decision to get chicks, we ordered a few from a Vermont feed store, but the heirloom poultry we ordered from the Murray McMurray Hatchery in Texas. If you don't know Murray McMurray Hatchery, you're in for a treat. It has the kind of catalog that gives bathroom reading a good name.

Our first question was: How many chickens should we get? We always assume that we'll lose a few to predators and have found that ten hens keep a family of four in eggs, with an occasional surplus dozen that our son, Trainer, and more recently our daughter, Isabel, can sell. Plus, we never eat our hens, so inevitably a few in our flock are old and no longer prodigious layers. We've had as many as 12, which was a bit much, and as few as 3, which didn't seem like a flock. You must order a minimum of 25 chicks, which enables McMurray to squeeze them together in a straw-lined, perforated crate, keeping them warm and snug while they are shipped overnight. If that's too many chicks for you, find a friend to team up with or order from a company that sells smaller amounts.

I was as nervous as, well, a mother hen preparing for them. First I had to find a box (a *brooder*, in chicks lingo) to keep them in for that first month, when they'd live in our mudroom. Who knew that in these days of recycling boxes one would be surprisingly difficult to come by? Stores flatten and dispose of them almost immediately. I tried several furniture stores, feeling like Goldilocks: Sorry, the La-Z-Boy box is too big, the lamp box is too small. A nice man at the Vermont Furniture Store suggested we come at a precise time — when the truck was unloading merchandise, before the boxes were carted away — and the kids and I ended up doing so, fishing through the gigantic Dumpster for one.

Next I brooded about the heat lamp, which we ended up jerry-rigging from a pole nailed to two doorposts in our mudroom. Would I cook them if the lamp hung too low? Would they freeze if it was too high? Trainer hunted for the perfect stick in the woods, and we poked it through the box to make a perch. We picked up

chicken feed and a waterer and put them in place, along with a nest of newspapers and pine shavings. The anticipation was as sweet as setting up a nursery. We were ready.

The Wednesday before Easter, I was awakened by a call from the Williamstown post office at 5:30 A.M. announcing that my chicks had arrived. I scrambled to get dressed quickly. My babies were waiting and probably hungry. When I walked into the post office 15 minutes later, the big marbled room silent save for the sound of my shoes clicking on the polished floor, the postman opened the door from the basement and suddenly I heard a choir of peepers.

I was enchanted by their cuteness — only 2 days old, they could easily have fit inside an egg — though their utter fragility just below the feathers' fluffiness when we cupped them in our hands was unnerving. Beneath a façade of feathers was incredible boniness; there was no fat, no muscle. They were like miniature dinosaurs with outsized personalities. I was reminded of the pink and blue Easter chicks I'd received as a child and how my mother let them "free range" in our coastal Maine kitchen. She fenced them in with a baby gate, and they would perch on the warm door pedal of our refrigerator. Once they started flying, we took them to a chicken farm that had a flock of pink and blue chickens. The memory reminds me of Gary Larson's drawing of a boneless chicken ranch, with a bunch of limp chickens hanging around.

Having young chicks is a wonderful opportunity to teach your children a bit about livestock handling. Trainer and Isabel showed the babies how to drink and perch and where to eat. They knew that the more they bonded with the chicks — talking and cooing to them, cradling them — the more responsive and familial the hens would be to them as they grew. The girls are their pets. Baby chicks have provided countless hours of entertainment in our mudroom, for both our kids and their friends and, if truth be told, the adults. I love to come down in the morning to hear a chorus of peeping, and the last thing I do before I go to bed is check in on them, all nestled together, asleep. After a few basic lessons in handling and hygiene, such as always washing your hands before and after holding them and how not to drop them, even preschoolers can take part in their care.

The chicks camped out happily in our mudroom for their first few months, but with warm weather approaching, the coop started to beckon. They go from fluffballs to actual birds pretty quickly. Their dust is everywhere. They want to explore. Indeed, it didn't occur to us to put a screen over the top of the box (who knew chickens could fly?) until one night, when Joe and I were watching a movie, we saw a chick strutting by the living room door. She took one look at us and kept on going.

It wasn't until after we'd had chickens for about a year and started to experiment with recipes for all those eggs that we realized another dividend of having your own hens: eggs from your own hens, with proper care, can be eaten raw. Slowly it dawned on us that the coast was clear to resurrect those marvelous classic recipes that had all but vanished in recent years. Hollandaise sauce. Caesar salad. Real smoothies.

Up until a few years ago, it was still a tradition at the finest restaurants in Manhattan for a chef to make a Caesar salad at your table with flair and showmanship. Now you're lucky if a restaurant makes its own croutons (you *know* they don't make the dressing), and what passes for Caesar salad is a poor impostor. *Et tu, Brute?* With your own eggs, hail Caesar!

JOE'S CAESAR SALAD

INGREDIENTS

1 garlic clove, peeled

¼ cup extra-virgin olive oil

1 French baguette, cut into ¾-inch cubes

1 egg

Juice from ½ lemon

1 tablespoon white wine vinegar

4–8 oil-packed anchovy fillets, diced

2–3 dashes Worcestershire sauce

2 heads romaine lettuce

½ cup freshly grated Parmesan cheese

Freshly ground black pepper

Serves 4 as a side dish, 2 as a main dish

We have a tradition in our household of trying to perfect a recipe. One winter I made a different apple pie every weekend for six weeks. The variations weren't dramatic (after all, how many ingredients can go into an apple pie?) but there were distinct, albeit subtle, differences. Each person in my family voted for his or her favorite, and the winner is still the pie I make, to rave reviews, all the time.

When we started getting eggs from our hens, Joe went on a mission to make the best Caesar salad, experimenting with many variations. This is his amazing result. As is true for all simple recipes, use only the finest ingredients, especially olive oil and Parmesan, for best results.

. . . .

HOW TO MAKE

1 Slice the garlic clove in half. Rub a large wooden bowl with the halves, then mince the garlic with a press.

2 Heat 2 tablespoons of the oil in a medium skillet over medium heat. Add the garlic and sauté until browned. Add the bread cubes and sauté until browned and crisp. Set aside the skillet of croutons.

3 Bring a small saucepan of water to a boil over medium-high heat. Boil the egg for 60 seconds, then cool under running water. Crack the egg into a small bowl, scraping out any egg white that clings to the shell. Add the lemon juice, the remaining 2 tablespoons of oil, the vinegar, the anchovies, and the Worcestershire and whisk together for the dressing.

4 Slice the romaine crosswise into ½-inch strips. (Romaine should be crisp. If yours is not, soak it in ice water for 5 minutes.) Toss the lettuce with the dressing in the prepared wooden bowl. Top with the croutons, Parmesan, and generous amounts of black pepper. (The anchovies will add quite a bit of salt, so you likely will not need to add more.) Serve immediately.

CREAMY ITALIAN DRESSING

INGREDIENTS

½ cup mayonnaise (recipe follows)

1 small garlic clove, minced

1 small shallot, minced

1 tablespoon red wine vinegar

½ teaspoon sugar

1 teaspoon minced fresh flat-leaf parsley

¼ teaspoon dried thyme

¼ teaspoon salt

Freshly ground black pepper

Makes ½ cup

When I was growing up, in the 1970s, my mother had eight or nine basic dinner recipes that she kept rotating: meatballs on Monday, roast beef on Sunday, chicken cacciatore on special occasions. We'd have fish in the summer when my dad caught it, and scallops from Buzzards Bay in the fall. My mother was nurturing, but she never really embraced cooking (even though in her later years she liked to cook), partly because to her it was a symbol of women being pigeonholed into a domestic role and also because if she had free time, she much preferred to read. But she always made her own salad dressings, rubbing her wooden salad bowl with garlic for that extra flavor.

. . . .

HOW TO MAKE

Combine the mayonnaise, garlic, shallot, vinegar, sugar, parsley, thyme, and salt in a small bowl and mix until well blended. Season with pepper to taste. Store in the refrigerator and use within a few days.

Phrases with a Ring of Truth

+ not all it's cracked up to be
+ rule the roost
+ clucking
+ henpecked
+ coming home to roost
+ cooped up
+ nesting instinct
+ not a peep
+ pecking order
+ flew the coop
+ coddled

MAYONNAISE

INGREDIENTS

½ cup canola oil

½ cup extra-virgin olive oil

1 egg

¼ teaspoon dry mustard

¼ teaspoon salt

1 tablespoon lemon juice,
  plus more if needed

Makes 1 cup

The exact origins of mayonnaise are uncertain, but it may have been created by a French duke's chef in 1756, while the word *mayonnaise* may derive from the medieval French word *moyeu*, which means "yolk of an egg." Taking fewer than 10 minutes to prepare, this is the true Miracle Whip. An emulsion of egg yolks and oil, mayonnaise can be embellished with all sorts of seasonings: garlic, chives, a teaspoon of curry powder, or a few anchovy fillets. Fresh mayonnaise will transform an egg salad sandwich and will keep in the refrigerator for up to 1 week.

· ·

HOW TO MAKE

1 Combine the canola oil and olive oil in a measuring cup.

2 Break the egg into a blender, add the mustard and salt, cover, and blend at top speed until the mixture is thick and foamy, about 3 seconds. Add the lemon juice and blend for 10 seconds. With the blender on high speed, slowly add the combined oils, a drop at a time. If you find the mayonnaise gets too thick, add a few more drops of lemon juice.

☺ Egg Safety

In many ways, rotten eggs are a thing of the past ("Last one in's a rotten egg!"), due to superior refrigeration techniques. Most people know to keep store-bought eggs refrigerated, and my advice to be on the safe side is to refrigerate the eggs from your own hens, too. If I'm making a dish in the evening and collecting eggs in the morning, I'll lay them on the counter until I cook them, because I love looking at them and a few hours at room temperature doesn't matter. But if I'm not using eggs within a day, I'll refrigerate them.

Be mindful of the fact, though, that once you refrigerate them, they'll need to be kept refrigerated. Fresh unwashed eggs have a protective coating that seals the pores naturally to inhibit bacteria. Those you buy in a store should be refrigerated because factories use a chemical wash to clean the eggs, which inadvertently also cleans off this secretion that coats and protects the egg from surface bacteria until it's ready to hatch. Sometimes my son Trainer's customers complain that the eggs he sells aren't entirely clean, and he explains that it is actually an advantage — rinsing an egg also makes a shell permeable to smells.

To determine whether an egg is fresh, you can do the old "sink-or-swim" test. Drop an egg gently into a glass of salted water. If it's up to 3 days old, it will sink to the bottom. As an egg ages, it will gather more air and float halfway up the water; if an egg floats horizontally on top of the surface, pitch it. (And while we're on housekeeping hints: Always wash your hands after handling the shells.)

Eggs should be used within a month (though you need to use your judgment on this), and are best stored unwashed, with the pointed end down (so the yolk, which will float to the top, has plenty of room) in a crate or receptacle that allows air to circulate. Interestingly, in terms of cooking, eggs separate best when cold and blend best when at room temperature.

When using eggs raw, I wash the eggs just before cracking them. Because I know my coop is clean and rodent free, and my chickens are healthy, I feel much better about eating the eggs from my backyard raw than I would be about eating supermarket eggs raw. But if you are young, elderly, or have a health condition, or have questions about consuming raw eggs, you should talk with your doctor first. Most of the recipes in this chapter, as well as the ice cream and sherbet recipes (see pages 166–170) in the desserts chapter, are made with raw eggs.

HOLLANDAISE SAUCE

INGREDIENTS

½ cup (1 stick) butter

3 egg yolks

2 tablespoons lemon juice, plus more if needed

½ teaspoon salt

Pinch of cayenne or freshly ground black or white pepper

Makes ¾ cup

The rawer the egg, the closer you are to a perfect egg experience healthwise, tastewise, even aesthetics-wise. Hollandaise sauce approaches that. It's delicious drizzled over steamed asparagus, poached salmon, or eggs Benedict, which my kids get a kick out of, given that we're related to Benedict Arnold. (My grandmother always pointed out that we're descended from the Benedict Arnold who was governor of Rhode Island in 1663; Benedict Arnold the traitor was a childless cousin.) But we're no relation to the dish, which was purportedly named after Lemuel Benedict, a Wall Street broker in the 1890s who suggested the recipe to a chef at the Waldorf Hotel in New York as a hangover cure.

HOW TO MAKE

1 Melt the butter in a small saucepan over low heat. Do not allow it to brown.

2 Combine the egg yolks, lemon juice, salt, and cayenne in a blender and process until blended. With the blender running, slowly add the butter, drop by drop, and then in a thin stream as the sauce thickens and emulsifies. Taste then add more lemon juice, if desired. Serve immediately, while still warm.

BÉARNAISE SAUCE

Béarnaise is in the same family as hollandaise, and both are mayonnaise's creamy cousins. This sauce also uses the technique of emulsifying warm butter with egg yolks. Béarnaise gains its independence from hollandaise by having vinegar instead of lemon, plus tarragon. It is a great enhancer of grilled meats and fish.

INGREDIENTS

- 2 tablespoons champagne or white wine vinegar
- 2 tablespoons dry white wine, plus more if needed (optional)
- 3 shallots, minced
- 2 tablespoons chopped fresh tarragon leaves
  - Freshly ground black or white pepper
- ¾ cup (1½ sticks) butter
- 3 egg yolks, at room temperature
  - Kosher salt

Makes about 1 cup

HOW TO MAKE

1 Bring to a boil the vinegar, wine, shallots, 1 tablespoon of the tarragon, and pepper to taste in a saucepan over medium heat, then simmer until reduced to a few tablespoons, 5 to 8 minutes. While it is cooling, melt the butter in a small saucepan over low heat, being careful not to let it brown or boil.

2 Combine the egg yolks and the vinegar mixture in a blender, then slowly add the hot butter in a drizzle. Season with salt and the remaining 1 tablespoon of tarragon, blending for a second or two. If the sauce is too thick, thin with a few more drops of white wine or water. Serve immediately.

"An egg of one hour old, bread of one day, a goat of one month, wine of six months, flesh of a year, fish of ten years and a wife of twenty years, a friend among a hundred, are the best of all number."

— John Wodroephe, *Spared Hours* (1623)

BANANA SMOOTHIE

1 banana

1 cup milk

1 egg

1 teaspoon ground flaxseed

1 teaspoon vanilla extract

Serves 1

When my kids come home from school starving, I serve this healthy snack, which is made sweet by the bananas. They are quite suspicious if I add flaxseed to their cereal, but in a smoothie they never notice. This recipe is also a handy way to use up ripe bananas, and adding the egg is an especially good way for me to get extra protein into my vegetarian son's diet. You can embellish this recipe any number of ways; try adding different fruits or ice cream, for example.

HOW TO MAKE

Combine the banana, milk, egg, flaxseed, and vanilla in a blender and blend on high speed until smooth. Serve immediately.

MANGO SMOOTHIE

INGREDIENTS

2 cups fresh or frozen peeled, pitted, and chopped mango

1 cup milk

1 egg

1 teaspoon ground flaxseed

1 cup ice cubes

Freshly grated nutmeg

Serves 2

I've got a mango kid: Isabel can't get enough of them. In my humble opinion, fresh mangoes are best served while wearing a bathing suit on a palm-fringed tropical island, standing knee-deep in aqua waves where you can suck contentedly on the messy fruit, but a smoothie may be the next best thing. I think these are plenty sweet, but if you've got a sweet tooth, experiment by adding a bit of honey or sugar or a dollop of vanilla ice cream.

HOW TO MAKE

Combine the mango, milk, egg, and flaxseed in a blender and blend briefly. Add the ice and blend briefly. Dust the top with nutmeg and serve.

PRAIRIE OYSTER

INGREDIENTS

1 teaspoon Worcestershire sauce

1 tablespoon tomato juice

1 egg yolk

1–2 dashes Tabasco sauce

Salt and freshly ground black pepper

Serves 1

Not for the faint of heart, the prairie oyster is thought to be good for what ails you after a night of hard drinking. "A month ago," bragged James Bond in *Thunderball*, "there wasn't a week went by but that on at least one day I couldn't eat anything for breakfast but a couple of aspirins and a prairie oyster. . . ."

• •

HOW TO MAKE

Pour the Worcestershire, tomato juice, egg yolk, and Tabasco, in that order, into an old-fashioned glass (taking care not to break the yolk). Sprinkle with salt and pepper and drink in one gulp.

"It is the Worcestershire sauce that gives it its color. The raw egg makes it nutritious. The red pepper gives it its bite. Gentlemen have told me they have found it extremely invigorating after a late evening."

— the butler Jeeves
in P. G. Wodehouse's *Jeeves Takes Charge*

Grinding Your Own

Like many other spices, as long as the nut remains whole, the aroma and flavor of the nutmeg is locked inside; once it is ground, it loses its potency quickly. It's worth the teeny bit of effort (and it is teeny) to grind your own nutmeg, for both the robust flavor and the smell. I keep whole nutmeg and a mini grater on a shelf next to the ingredients I use on a daily basis. I grate it onto all sorts of things: eggnog, Grape-Nuts pudding, oatmeal, apple pie, French toast, and so on. Whole nutmeg and mini graters can be found at a gourmet cooking store.

EGGNOG

INGREDIENTS

4 eggs, at room temperature, separated

½–¾ cup sugar

2 cups milk (whole or low-fat)

1 cup heavy cream or whole milk

1 teaspoon vanilla extract

Rum, bourbon, or brandy (optional)

Freshly grated nutmeg

Serves 4

In seventeenth-century England, eggnog was served by landed gentry in the days before refrigeration, when eggs and milk were luxuries, as a rare holiday toast to one's health. The "nog" may derive from an ancient English word referring to a small vessel used to serve alcohol. It's delicious as is, or spiked with rum, bourbon, or brandy.

HOW TO MAKE

1 Beat the egg yolks with the sugar in a large bowl until blended. Stir in the milk, cream, and vanilla.

2 In a separate bowl, beat the egg whites until stiff peaks form, then fold them thoroughly into the milk mixture. Pour into glasses: add a bit of rum, if desired; sprinkle with nutmeg; and serve.

Note: Alternatively, combine the milk, cream, and vanilla in a heavy saucepan and slowly heat until hot but not boiling. Beat the eggs in a bowl with the sugar, then slowly add half the hot milk mixture, whisking constantly. Pour the mixture back into the saucepan and cook on medium heat until it begins to thicken. Remove from the heat and chill. Add the rum, if desired, and nutmeg to individual servings.

Location, Location, Location

Our coop is on the edge of our lawn, where the yard meets the woods. We can see the hens from the house and call to them from the driveway. Our coop's location for us was dictated by convenience. We had a decrepit shed already — sort of a coop *disgrace* that we fixed up — but if you're starting from scratch, the location is something to consider. The hens have decimated the grassy area that used to be part of our lawn and is now their pen; it's a hardscrabble area with crater marks from their digging that looks as if Charlie Brown's friend Pig-Pen lives there. On the days we let them out of the fenced area to roam the yard, they head for my garden and try to eat my prettiest flower buds. They always go for my parsley. They poop on the porch steps. But we love them.

CHICKS WHO RIP

Breakfast

"Truly, thou art dammed like an ill roasted egg, all on one side."

— William Shakespeare, *As You Like It*

The name of this chapter comes from a bumper sticker that my 14-year-old niece, Abby, sent me from Kauai. Chicks Who Rip was the name of a Hawaiian surf shop started by a fellow who wanted to create a line of clothing for women and girls who are active and love to surf (*rip* means to play hard and well). Chickens are similarly feisty, and the bumper sticker stuck, on the door to the coop.

As soon as our chickens were big enough to take the chilly New England evenings, at about 10 weeks, we introduced them to their coop. When they were around 25 weeks, they started laying their first eggs (called pullet eggs), which are small and sometimes unevenly colored or shaped. Prized by gourmands, pullets sell for about $10 a dozen in fancy places like Dean & Deluca and the Union Square Greenmarket, but who would want to sell them? The first egg is a pleasure to behold.

When our first hen laid her first egg, I think she was as startled as I when she just dropped it unceremoniously in the yard. I saw it in the dirt in a little hollowed-out area under the ramp to the coop. I shouted out loud and startled her; we'd been looking for one for days. It reminded me of when I was a kid and my father decided to grow tomato plants from seed. He tended them assiduously and watched them grow, and by early summer every day after work he'd hurry out to the backyard before he even changed out of his tie, looking for signs of a tomato. One day he came home and found big beefsteak tomatoes on the vine — he shouted to us to come see! Then he noticed our neighbor leaning over the fence chuckling, and we looked down and saw they were tied onto his plants with twist ties. We all thought it was hilarious.

Birds to Raise for Their Breed Names Alone

+ Buttercup
+ Cuckoo Maran
+ Golden Pencil Hamburg
+ Golden Sex Link
+ Polish Frizzle
+ Top Hat Special

We put some Easter eggs into the coop to encourage the system, and they caught on. We soon had many eggs, and when we started dreaming up new ways to cook them, we realized their extraordinary versatility and their deliciousness in many forms, from a sunny little egg served simply for breakfast before my kids get on the bus to an exquisite poached queen that rides into a dinner party on a bed of wild mushroom ragout, laced with truffle oil. Long the staple of farms that are too often short of cash, eggs can signify luxury or austerity: The favorite dish of England's King Charles II was eggs with ambergris (produced in the digestive system of a sperm whale), whereas my mother grew up one of six kids in the Depression on a diet of eggs and could never eat quiche again.

And their disguises? My Norwegian friends Hanne and Geir, upon arriving in the United States as university students, could barely get through breakfast in any diner, so bewildering were the language and the seemingly unending array of egg choices on the menu: scrambled, sunny-side up, over easy, over light, poached, hard-boiled, fried, baked, shirred, or Benedict (what? wasn't that a guy? what a betrayal). And that's just breakfast. With their exquisite response to subtle heat changes, eggs lend themselves to more personality than Cher's wardrobe, being puffed into lemony soufflés, shaken into omelets, poured into frittatas, baked inside tomatoes, dropped into soups, whipped into meringues, or served up raw in steak tartare.

But it all starts with breakfast.

BACKYARD CHICKEN
FAQs

Do the eggs taste different in the winter, when chickens can't forage for grubs and bugs in the heavy snow? To tell you the truth, I haven't noticed a difference. We still feed our hens food scraps daily, so they have a varied diet. (And as I write this in midwinter, I've just finished shoveling snow to form a path for the hens from their ramp to the scraps, since they stand in the entranceway, take one look at the snow, shudder, and refuse to go out.)

Do the chickens produce the same number of eggs throughout the year? We get a lot fewer eggs in the winter. Even if I put a heat lamp in the coop, which I do when it gets below 20°F (–7°C) — they are birds, after all, with feathers, designed to be outdoors, but I'm a softie when it gets frigid — the egg production falls off. We definitely have more quiches and lemon meringue pies in warmer months.

How easy is it to keep chickens? This is perhaps the question I'm asked the most, especially by people contemplating chickens. The answer is: Very easy. In the morning, one of our kids opens the coop door on his or her way to school and turns off their night-light. We keep a pot on the stove to collect food scraps, and when we think of it or when the pot gets full, we toss the scraps into their yard. In the evening, when it gets dark, Trainer closes the coop door, collects the eggs, and turns on their light. Period.

We replenish their water and grain typically once a week. If we go away on vacation, either a friend who likes fresh eggs performs this twice-daily ritual or we ask a kid in the neighborhood. If we go away overnight, we'll sometimes leave them in the coop with the door closed, where they'll be safe. In the winter, when it's snowy, they'll go for days without being outside anyway. Twice a year we clean the coop. That's pretty much it. Of course, you can play with them, or let them run free around the yard, but they are perfectly content to just hang out with each other, too.

SOFT-BOILED EGG

1 egg, at room temperature

Serves 1

You wouldn't think it's easy to go wrong with eggs. As *The Picayune Creole Cook Book* of 1928 noted tartly, "A chapter on eggs would be superfluous in any cook book, were it not for the fact that there are women who cannot tell to a real certainty how to boil an egg soft or hard, when the omelet is cooked to a nicety, and how to send to the table in all the perfection of good cooking that most delicate and palatable dish, scrambled eggs." The authors went on to note that Creoles "wisely eschew" all innovations in eggs that call for them to be cooked for more than 8 minutes, for good reason, concluding that eggs "cannot be too highly recommended to delicate persons, to hard brain workers, and to families generally." Though I don't suggest following their advice for root beer, which they made with filtered swamp water, they knew a thing or two about eggs. This recipe is for a soft-cooked egg, with a firm egg white and a runny yolk.

HOW TO MAKE

Put the egg in a small saucepan and add water to barely cover. Bring to a boil, then immediately reduce the heat and simmer for 4 minutes for a medium egg or 6 minutes for a large egg. Remove the egg with a slotted spoon and run cold water over it to cool it slightly. Crack and serve.

"There is something about cold weather that leads to reflective searchings back through memory and time, to dishes sprung from the farthest reaches of childhood, to nursery foods, odd, peculiar little dishes in which one crumbled crackers in warm milk or probed bread fingers into a soft-boiled egg."

— Judith Olney

SOFT-BOILED EGG, TAKE TWO

4 eggs

Chopped fresh chives

Kosher salt and freshly ground black pepper

Serves 2

My friend Jody Fijal learned this technique from a cooking class she took at a German restaurant in the Berkshires, where they served these eggs in martini glasses with mother-of-pearl spoons (to eliminate any metallic taste in the eggs).

. . . .

HOW TO MAKE

Bring a saucepan of water to a boil, then submerge the eggs, immediately reduce to a simmer, and cook for 5 minutes. Remove and place in a bowl or sink full of water with lots of ice for 30 seconds. Believe it or not, you can then crack the tip and peel a soft-boiled egg carefully. Serve two in a martini glass with chopped chives and a bit of salt and pepper.

MEDIUM-BOILED EGG

INGREDIENT

1 egg, at room temperature

Serves 1

When we started getting eggs from our hens, I gravitated toward simple recipes. I didn't want them disguised inside a cake; I wanted to see them, in all their glory. I was so proud of our hens. This recipe makes an egg with a firm white and an egg yolk that's on the verge of solidifying.

. . . .

HOW TO MAKE

Put the egg in a small saucepan and add water to barely cover. Bring to a boil. Immediately reduce the heat and simmer for 6 minutes for a medium egg or 8 minutes for a large egg. Remove the egg with a slotted spoon and run cold water over it to cool. Crack and serve.

HARD-BOILED EGG

INGREDIENTS

12 eggs, at room temperature

Salt (optional)

Makes 12 eggs

Fresh eggs have many advantages, but easy peeling is not one of them; my first attempt to serve hard-boiled eggs resulted in pockmarked eggs that were missing half their whites. In this case, older is better. As an egg ages, it loses moisture through its thousands of pores, causing the egg to shrink and the egg white to stick less to the membrane. If you're hard-boiling eggs, stick a dozen fresh eggs in the back of your refrigerator for a week or two before cooking them. Another tip is to boil your eggs quickly and plunge them into an ice bath after cooking. Hard-boiled eggs will keep in the shell refrigerated for up to 1 week.

HOW TO MAKE

In a pan large enough to hold the eggs generously, boil enough water to cover the eggs. Add salt to the boiling water, if desired. Gently slide in the eggs. Boil for 10 to 15 minutes, depending on the consistency you prefer and the size of your eggs. (The shorter amount of time gives you a solidified egg white but leaves the egg yolk a bit soft. The longer cooking time guarantees a traditional hard-boiled egg.) Drain the water from the eggs, then plunge them into a bowl or sink full of ice water until the eggs have cooled completely.

"Being kissed by a man who didn't wax his moustache was like eating an egg without salt."

— Rudyard Kipling, *The Story of the Gadsbys*

SHIRRED EGGS

These are dressed-up soft-boiled eggs that are cooked in a buttered dish under the broiler. In France, this method of baking eggs is called *oeufs en cocotte*, which means "eggs baked in ramekins." Do try them — they're delicious, elegant, and easy.

. . . .

INGREDIENTS

2 teaspoons minced mixed fresh herbs (such as flat-leaf parsley, thyme, basil, or chives)

1 tablespoon freshly grated Parmesan cheese

Salt and freshly ground black or white pepper

½ teaspoon butter, melted

2 teaspoons heavy cream

2 eggs

Serves 1

HOW TO MAKE

1 Set an oven rack 8 inches from the broiler and preheat.

2 Combine the herbs, Parmesan, and salt and pepper to taste in a small bowl.

3 Brush the butter over the bottom of a small ovenproof ramekin large enough to hold the eggs side by side, and then pour a little ribbon of cream around the edge. Break the eggs on top of the butter, one beside the other. Sprinkle the eggs with the herb mixture.

4 Broil about 6 minutes, until the whites are set but the yolks are still runny. Serve immediately.

PERFECT POACHED EGG

INGREDIENTS

Pinch of salt

1 teaspoon rice vinegar

1 egg

Serves 1

In ancient Rome, most meals began with an egg, the shell of which was crushed into the dish to prevent evil spirits from lurking. When I was a kid, my father would serve poached eggs in a teacup with a dab of butter, a shake of pepper, and bacon crumbled on top. Or, for a Sunday-night-supper treat, my mother would cook one on corned beef hash right from the can that she had crisped to perfection in her skillet. Poached eggs can save you on a busy night when you need a meal fast: you can add a poached egg to a bowl of soup, a plate of steamed vegetables, or a salad. It's a marvel to consider, in shape, texture, and taste.

. . . .

HOW TO MAKE

1 Fill a saucepan or skillet with enough water to cover your egg, then bring to a boil. Add a pinch of salt and the vinegar (which will help keep the egg whole) and reduce to a simmer.

2 Crack the egg into a saucer or small bowl, then gently slide the egg into the water (holding the saucer at the water's edge). Use a spoon to nudge the white closer to the yolk.

3 Turn off the heat, cover, and let sit for 3 minutes. Remove the egg from the saucepan with a slotted spoon, trim any ragged edges, and serve.

"Whipped cream isn't whipped cream at all if it hasn't been whipped with whips, just like poached eggs isn't poached eggs unless it's been stolen in the dead of the night."

— Roald Dahl

SCRAMBLED EGGS

INGREDIENTS

4 eggs

4–6 tablespoons milk or cream

1–2 teaspoons butter

Salt and freshly ground black pepper

1 teaspoon chopped fresh chives, scallions, thyme, or flat-leaf parsley

Grated cheese, such as cheddar or Parmesan (optional)

Serves 2

Hint: If you've ever found yourself scrambling to make toast and cook eggs at the same time, try this: When the eggs look wet but are no longer liquid, turn off the heat and gently pile the eggs into the center of the skillet, leaving the skillet on the burner. Go make your toast, then serve the perfectly cooked eggs.

How can you mess up scrambled eggs? It's not so hard; they can easily become dry. The secret is a low fire and plenty of stirring. Adding a bit of milk or cream or even water yields a fluffier, creamier dish. Because my husband is a museum director, we do our fair share of entertaining. Sometimes, instead of inviting artists or visiting collectors to dinner, we'll have them over for Sunday breakfast, introducing them first to the hens, then dishing up fresh scrambled eggs and toast with our kids at our big kitchen table that Joe made. Truth be told, it's sometimes more relaxing to entertain at breakfast than at dinner, when the expectations (the food, the wine, the kids' behavior!) are higher.

HOW TO MAKE

1 Crack the eggs into a medium bowl. Add the milk and whisk vigorously.

2 Heat a pat of butter in a skillet over medium heat. When the butter begins to sizzle, pour in the egg mixture and reduce the heat to low. Once the liquid has started to set, add salt and pepper to taste, chives, cheese (if using), and anything else you'd like, folding them in gently with a wooden spoon. Stir constantly, gently scraping the eggs from the edge of the skillet to the center, until your eggs have the consistency you desire. Serve immediately.

SCRAMBLED EGGS WITH LINGUIÇA & CHEDDAR CHEESE

INGREDIENTS

2 ounces linguiça or chorizo, finely chopped (about ½ cup)

½ cup diced green bell pepper

4 scallions, thinly sliced

10 eggs

1 cup shredded sharp cheddar cheese (4 ounces)

Kosher or sea salt and freshly ground black pepper

¼ cup chopped fresh cilantro leaves

Serves 5

Growing up near the fishing port of New Bedford, Massachusetts, where a lot of people of Portuguese descent live, we'd often find linguiça on diner menus, in the grocery store, and at street fairs. I've always loved its piquant, slightly greasy flavor. When I first got out of college and spent a winter living near New Bedford writing feature stories for the *New Bedford Standard Times*, I'd grill it with green bell peppers and onions on my little hibachi, toss it into a Portuguese bun with a little mustard, and wash it down with beer.

This dish is adapted from a recipe from my cookbook-writing friend Jeanne Besser, who uses the meat to put a spin on traditional Western omelet flavors. If you have leftover cooked potatoes, dice them up and sauté them with the bell peppers. Serve with Portuguese bread, tortillas, English muffins, or whole-wheat toast.

● ●

HOW TO MAKE

1 Sauté the linguiça in a large nonstick skillet over medium heat until it renders some of its fat, 3 to 5 minutes. Add the bell pepper and scallions and sauté until just softened, 3 to 5 minutes.

2 Beat the eggs in a medium bowl, then add them to the skillet and cook, stirring until the eggs are scrambled and just beginning to set. Add the cheese and stir to combine. Cook until the eggs are still soft but no longer runny. Be careful not to overcook. Season with salt and pepper and serve immediately, topped with the cilantro.

SCRAMBLED EGGS, INDIAN-STYLE

INGREDIENTS

4 eggs

2 tablespoons extra-virgin olive oil

½ yellow onion, chopped (about ¼ cup)

1 small tomato, chopped

1 green chile, seeded and slivered (or substitute 1 teaspoon chili powder)

1 tablespoon chopped fresh cilantro

¼ teaspoon minced garlic

¼ teaspoon minced fresh ginger

Salt and freshly ground black pepper

¼ teaspoon toasted cumin seed

Pinch of ground turmeric

Serves 2

When I was in my early twenties, I lived on 6th Street in New York's East Village, where within one block there were six Indian restaurants. My parents would come down and take a gang of us out to dinner, my father always amazed that the bill came to less than $50. Walking home many evenings from work, I'd swing along 6th Street between First and Second Avenues, loving the aroma of garlic, ginger, and other fragrances wafting from the basement restaurants. You might serve these eggs with toast, paratha, or roti, or turn the dish into a light supper with rice. If you have leftover roasted chicken, you could also shred a bit and add it to the dish. These scrambled eggs also make a good sandwich filling.

HOW TO MAKE

1 Beat the eggs and set aside.

2 Heat the oil in a medium skillet over medium heat. Add the onion and cook until translucent, 2 or 3 minutes. Add the tomato, chile, cilantro, garlic, and ginger and cook until the tomato is soft (so you can mash it). Season with salt and pepper, the cumin seed, and the turmeric.

3 Pour in the eggs and scramble until they reach the desired consistency. Serve immediately.

HUEVOS RANCHEROS WITH TWO SALSAS

INGREDIENTS

2 cups cooked black beans (see Note), seasoned with 1 minced jalapeño chile, 1 minced garlic clove, 1 teaspoon ground coriander, and salt

1 ripe Hass avocado, pitted, peeled, and diced

5 scallions, chopped

2 tablespoons chopped fresh cilantro

2 tablespoons El Yucateco or other green hot sauce

1 tablespoon vegetable oil, or more as needed

8 (6-inch) corn tortillas

8 eggs

2 cups shredded Monterey jack or cheddar cheese

1½ cups Tomato Salsa (recipe follows)

Serves 4

A classic Mexican breakfast, huevos rancheros ("ranchers' eggs") are fried eggs served on corn tortillas and smothered in salsa. I first tried them in an all-night diner after a late night of music in Austin and found them divine. El Yucateco is a habanero-based sauce that can be found in grocery stores; if you can't find it, substitute another simple hot sauce that uses the fiery habanero chile.

. . . .

HOW TO MAKE

1 Preheat the broiler.

2 Heat the beans and set aside. Combine the avocado, scallions, cilantro, and hot sauce to make a green salsa; set aside.

3 Heat the oil (just enough to coat the pan — it may be more than 1 tablespoon) in a large skillet. Heat each tortilla briefly on both sides in the hot oil, just long enough to soften and heat through. Transfer to paper towels to drain.

4 Fry the eggs any way you like them. While they are cooking, arrange two tortillas, side by side, on each ovenproof serving plate. Dollop some beans on each tortilla, then some cheese on top of the beans, and place the plates under the broiler to melt the cheese. Top each tortilla with an egg, plus a dollop of green salsa on one tortilla and a dollop of Tomato Salsa on the other. Serve immediately.

Note: You can cook your own beans or doctor up canned beans. To cook your own, wash and pick over 1 cup of dried beans, soak for 4 to 12 hours, then rinse. Put in a pot with 1 quart of cold water and bring to a boil, then simmer until tender, 1 to 2 hours, depending on the age of the beans and the altitude.

TOMATO SALSA

1 large ripe tomato, diced

½ small red onion, diced

½ jalapeño chile, seeded and minced

2–3 tablespoons chopped fresh cilantro

1 garlic clove, minced

Juice of 1 lime

2 tablespoons red hot sauce

Salt and freshly ground black pepper

Makes 1½ cups

The secret of great salsa resides in the ingredients, and particularly in using perfect tomatoes. If you like more heat, use an entire jalapeño, or even a habanero, or leave in the seeds (most of the heat of a chile is contained in the membrane that holds the seeds, as well as in the seeds). The beauty of the heat is that you can experiment. Add a little, taste, and add a little more if it's not zingy enough for your taste buds. This is a versatile recipe: if you substitute mango or papaya for the tomato, you'll have a jazzy fruit salsa that's a flavorful accent to grilled grouper or shrimp.

● ●

HOW TO MAKE

Combine the tomato, onion, jalapeño, cilantro, garlic, lime juice, hot sauce, and salt and pepper to taste in a small bowl. Store in the refrigerator and use within a few days.

"Noise proves nothing. Often a hen who has merely laid an egg cackles as if she laid an asteroid."

— Mark Twain

CORNED BEEF HASH & EGGS

INGREDIENTS

2 tablespoons butter

1 large yellow onion, chopped

1 red bell pepper, chopped

1 pound frozen hash browns (about 4 cups)

8 ounces thick-cut deli corned beef, cut into ¼-inch chunks (2 cups)

2 tablespoons chopped fresh flat-leaf parsley

Salt and freshly ground black pepper

4 eggs

Serves 4

My father was the weekend breakfast maker in our house, serving up pancakes or leftover steak and eggs and even designing menus for his concoctions. My mother got to sleep in while he and I watched *The Three Stooges*, then cooked breakfast. Corned beef hash and eggs — my father called them cackleberries — was a staple in the wintertime and is still a favorite of mine, served with ketchup.

. . . .

HOW TO MAKE

1 Melt the butter in a large nonstick skillet over medium heat and sauté the onion and bell pepper until soft, about 10 minutes. Stir in the hash browns and cook, stirring occasionally, until the potatoes begin to brown, about 20 minutes. Add the corned beef and cook until the potatoes are fully browned, for 20 minutes longer. Add the parsley and season with salt and pepper to taste.

2 Using the back of a spoon, make four shallow wells in the hash. One at a time, break the eggs into a shallow bowl and slip them into the wells. Increase the heat to medium, cover the skillet, and cook until the eggs are set, about 6 minutes (check frequently, as it happens fast). Serve immediately.

GREEN EGGS & HAM

People are amazed when they see the green eggs that our Araucana hen lays. In a nod to Dr. Seuss, here's a recipe that does turn out green eggs. An interesting aside: Dr. Seuss wrote the book on a bet with Bennett Cerf, his Random House editor, that he couldn't write a book using only 50 words. Seuss did it, and 49 of the words were one syllable.

. . . .

INGREDIENTS

4 slices ham (¼ inch thick)

¼ cup maple syrup

2 tablespoons red hot sauce

8 large eggs

⅓ cup milk

½ teaspoon salt

Freshly ground black pepper

3 scallions, chopped

2 tablespoons chopped fresh flat-leaf parsley

1 tablespoon green hot sauce

2 tablespoons butter

Serves 4

HOW TO MAKE

1 Preheat the broiler.

2 Place the ham in a broiler pan. Stir the maple syrup and red hot sauce together and pour over the ham.

3 Whisk the eggs, milk, salt, and pepper to taste in a large bowl. Add the scallions, parsley, and green hot sauce and blend.

4 Melt the butter in a large skillet over medium heat, then add the eggs. While you are scrambling the eggs, broil the ham, turning once so it colors on both sides. To serve, spoon some of the ham liquid on each plate and top with the ham and eggs.

"Nothing helps scenery like ham and eggs."
— Mark Twain

"A hen and a pig were sauntering down the main street of an Indiana town when they passed a restaurant that advertised 'Delicious ham and eggs: 75 cents.'

"'Sounds like a bargain,' approved the hen. 'That owner obviously knows how to run his business.'

"'It's all very well for you to be so pleased about the dish in question,' observed the pig with some resentment. 'For you it is all in the day's work. Let me point out, however, that on my part it represents a genuine sacrifice.'"

— Bennett Cerf

MIGAS

I first sampled *migas* ("crumbs" in Spanish) in Texas, where my brother-in-law Dave lives and knows the best roadhouses and restaurants. The dish is basically a Tex-Mex tangle of eggs, tortillas, and cheese. Serve it with warm flour tortillas, salsa, and sour cream. You can buy bottled tomatillo salsa but it's better fresh, and worth the little bit of effort.

INGREDIENTS

1 tablespoon butter

1½ cups Rustic Tomatillo Salsa (recipe follows)

1 tomato, diced

2 (6-inch) corn tortillas, cut into strips

Chopped green chiles (optional)

4 eggs, beaten and seasoned with salt and freshly ground black pepper

¼ cup crumbled queso fresco, goat cheese, or feta cheese

Serves 2

HOW TO MAKE

1 Heat the butter in a large nonstick skillet over medium heat. Add ½ cup of the salsa and the tomato and cook for 2 minutes. Add the tortilla strips and cook until softened, about 1 minute. Add the chiles, if using.

2 Pour in the eggs and as they start to set, pull them into the center of the pan, forming large curds. Continue pulling, lifting, and folding gently until thickened and no longer liquid. Remove from the heat and sprinkle with the cheese, stirring well to combine. Serve with the remaining 1 cup of salsa on the side.

RUSTIC TOMATILLO SALSA

INGREDIENTS

14 tomatillos, husked, washed, and coarsely chopped

1–2 serrano, jalapeño, or other chiles, chopped

1 small white onion, finely chopped

Juice of 1 lime

½ bunch fresh cilantro, chopped

½ teaspoon salt

Makes 2 cups

We belong to Caretaker Farm, a beautiful CSA (Community Supported Agriculture) farm in the Berkshires, and Isabel and I have our favorite times when we like to pick the vegetables. One is the beginning of September, when we run along the lane, past the chickens, across the brook, to the raspberry patch, where the berries are ripe and warm to the touch. (More make it into our mouths than into the pint crate.) Another is when the tomatillos are ready for picking. I love their secretive papery husk, which you peel off, and the slightly tart flavor they impart to a salsa.

• •

HOW TO MAKE

Combine the tomatillos, chiles, onion, lime juice, cilantro, and salt in a medium bowl (if you prefer a puréed salsa, blend in a food processor or blender). The salsa will keep in the refrigerator for a few days.

"She looks as new as a peeled egg."

— Dorothy Parker

 Really Free-Range?

I was suspicious of the buzzword *free-range*, which is today's "organic," and did learn that, although it's a fashionable term, it doesn't mean a whole lot. It signifies that a chicken has access to the outdoors, but that could be a 2- by 5-foot cement slab. If you care about such things, it's better to know the farm whence your chickens came.

CORN CAKES WITH POACHED EGGS & SALSA

INGREDIENTS

½ cup fresh or thawed frozen corn kernels

¼ cup yellow or white cornmeal

¼ cup unbleached all-purpose flour

½ teaspoon baking powder

½ teaspoon salt

1 egg

⅓ cup milk

1 tablespoon butter, melted and slightly cooled

1 tablespoon finely sliced fresh chives

4 poached eggs (see page 41), kept warm

Kosher or sea salt and freshly ground black pepper

½ cup salsa

¼ cup sour cream

½ Hass avocado, pitted, peeled, and sliced into 4 wedges

Serves 4

When our friends Jeanne and Richard Bessers visit, the chickens fascinate their son, Jack, who is willing to open up the coop and feed them even when it's snowing, which delights my kids to no end, sparing them that chore. Jeanne, a food writer for the *Atlanta Constitution*, and I enjoy cooking together. For those who have trouble deciding between eggs and pancakes for breakfast, this recipe of hers spares you from having to choose. A classic poached egg is perched on a chive-studded corn-cake base, then topped with salsa and sour cream.

HOW TO MAKE

1   Chop the corn coarsely. Combine the cornmeal, flour, baking powder, and salt in a large bowl. Beat the egg in another bowl. Add the milk and butter to the egg and stir to combine. Stir the egg mixture gently into the dry ingredients until just moistened. Gently stir in the corn and chives.

2   Heat a large nonstick or lightly greased griddle or skillet over high heat until a drop of water sizzles on the surface. Reduce the heat to medium. Divide the batter into four pancakes and cook the cakes until the bottoms are lightly golden, 1 to 2 minutes. Flip the cakes and cook the other side, 1 to 2 minutes.

3   Transfer each cake to a plate and top with a poached egg. Sprinkle with salt and pepper to taste. Spoon on some salsa and a dollop of sour cream, then add an avocado slice. Serve immediately.

CHALLAH FRENCH TOAST

INGREDIENTS

1 cup milk, half-and-half, or eggnog

4 eggs

1 teaspoon vanilla extract

Freshly grated nutmeg

Butter

1 loaf challah bread, sliced ¾–1 inch thick

Confectioners' sugar

Maple syrup

Fresh assorted berries (optional)

Serves 6–8

Note: If cooking these in batches, keep the cooked French toast warm in a 200°F oven.

Once upon a time, in the early 1980s, I lived on Manhattan's Lower East Side. It was a heady time: Blondie, Trash & Vaudeville, the Mud Club. By day I wrote my first book, about nuclear power, and by night I waitressed at the Kiev, a Ukrainian deli that was a fixture in the East Village.

At the Kiev when we weren't busy, I could use my high school Russian to chat with the dishwashers, who'd been college professors and teachers in the Ukraine, and it was there that I was turned on to challah bread, which is thick and eggy and makes perfect French toast. When I worked the midnight to 7 A.M. shift, I'd see all the characters who came in after a night of clubbing, craving coffee and a huge breakfast. I'll never forget the night I waited on a rocker who was as high as a kite. Moments after I served him French toast, he just conked out, like you see in the movies, falling facedown into the syrupy plate, the thick bread cushioning the blow. It didn't deter my love for this dish, though.

With this recipe, any bread will do, although stale, thick bread is best.

HOW TO MAKE

1 Whisk together the milk, eggs, vanilla, and nutmeg in a shallow bowl. Grease a large cast-iron skillet or griddle with the butter and set over medium heat.

2 Dip the bread in the egg mixture, swishing to coat on both sides, then let the excess drain off. Place the bread in the skillet, adding as many slices as will fit flat. Cook until deep golden brown on one side, 2 to 3 minutes, then flip and cook the other side until golden. Arrange on a platter, dust with confectioners' sugar, and serve with maple syrup and the fresh berries, if desired.

FRENCH GRIDDLE CAKES

Various forms of griddle cakes are found worldwide. This mini crêpe is served for breakfast or dessert. In late summer, when berries are abundant, you could substitute wild berries for the jelly.

. . . .

INGREDIENTS

6 eggs, separated

2 tablespoons sugar

1 cup sifted unbleached all-purpose flour

1 tablespoon butter, melted

1 cup milk, warmed

½ teaspoon baking powder

Butter

Jelly

Confectioners' sugar

Makes 60 small cakes

HOW TO MAKE

1 Beat the egg yolks with the sugar in a large bowl until light. Add the flour and melted butter, blend, and then add the warm milk. Beat until light.

2 Beat the egg whites into stiff peaks. Add the baking powder to the yolk mixture, then add the beaten egg whites. Beat until smooth.

3 Drop tablespoons of the batter onto a hot greased griddle set over medium heat, then turn quickly and cook the other side, 2 minutes total. Put on a plate, brush with butter and jelly, and dust with confectioners' sugar. Serve immediately.

HOT WHEELS

Lunch & Dinner

What did the Spanish farmer say to his chicken? Oh lay!

Our affectionate, animal-loving son, Trainer, was predisposed to loving chickens. At the age of eight he had already worked with the renowned Chinese artist Huang Yong Ping on an installation at MASS MoCA, where Joe and I have worked for over 20 years, that involved snakes, scorpions, millipedes, and tarantulas. I'll never forget his excited call from a herpetology store in New Hampshire. He'd been allowed to skip school and fly with his father and Huang Yong Ping to pick up the arachnids before the exhibition opened, and he reported to me breathlessly from his father's cell phone, "Mom, Dad said I can use my allowance to buy a pet *scorpion*!"

Terrific.

He did buy a scorpion, and after the exhibition opened at the museum, Trainer took the curator up on her offer to give him the job of feeding the snakes weekly. So, in third grade, every Monday after the museum closed he'd go to MASS MoCA and feed the snakes. Often his five-year-old sister, Isabel, would come along and he'd entertain her. I once walked into the galleries to see a baby boa curling its way up her arm, looking like an exotic bracelet except for the fact that it was actually a snake shinnying its way up under her T-shirt into her cute little armpit. Curator Susan Cross insisted the snake wouldn't hurt her, but my face must have registered the shock you're probably experiencing as you read these words, for Trainer gingerly took back the snake and returned it to the cage.

So taking care of the fairest fowl was a natural for Trainer, although, as he's approached his teenage years, it's not beyond him to take out the BB gun to stun hawks that hover menacingly around the coop. These girls were his pets from day one; he talked to them, coddled them, fed them, collected their eggs, and named each chick.

Harry Potter was named after both his grandfather, whose name was Harry Potter Trainer, and a favorite book character. There were Buffy and Orpy (our two Buff Orpingtons), and Chicken King, who reminded us of a fast-food joint we like in Vieques, Puerto Rico. My all-time favorite name, though, was Hot Wheels, who was a Rhode Island Red that tore around the yard.

On warm afternoons, Trainer would sit on the front porch with a chick perched on his shoulder, or he would send the hens into an ecstatic trance by turning them on their back and rubbing their feet and chest. I'd often let them run around the yard in the afternoon, and as he came up the driveway after the school bus dropped him off, they'd trot across the hilly yard to greet him.

One night, when the chicks were about a year old, Hot Wheels disappeared. Chickens are homebodies and will naturally return to the coop as dusk approaches (it's thought that birds lose their color vision at twilight, much earlier than do other animals), but this night Hot Wheels did not return. Our backyard is edged by a wooded slope that turns into the Appalachian Trail, and across the street from us is a river and railroad tracks, so the prospects weren't good. I had gone to an evening meeting and came home at 10 p.m. to find Joe sitting glumly at the kitchen table. "Hot Wheels is gone," he said. Trainer had gone to close the coop door when it got dark, counting the hens as he did every night, and came up one short. They hunted for her without luck, and eventually, inconsolable, Trainer had gone to bed. Joe didn't have the heart to tell him to go to sleep when he heard Trainer, long past his bedtime, calling futilely to the dark night air out his upstairs bedroom window, "Hooooot Wheels. Hooooooooot Wheeeeeels."

After I got home, Joe went out looking for her in the pouring rain. Later that evening, I pulled on my foul-weather gear and went out searching, combing the railroad tracks with a flashlight and calling out her name. No luck. It poured all night. In the morning, Joe got up early to check the road and tracks, thinking that at least he'd make sure the kids didn't see a flattened Hot Wheels while they waited for the bus. No sign of her. A half hour later, as we all ate breakfast silently at the kitchen table, who should come trotting up the driveway, head hunkered into her shoulders against the driving rain, but Hot Wheels. She'd made it through the night.

We all wondered what she'd seen.

FRIED EGG SANDWICH

INGREDIENTS

2 slices bacon, 1 sausage patty, or 1 slice Canadian bacon

1 teaspoon butter

1 egg

Salt and freshly ground black pepper

1 slice cheddar cheese

1 English muffin or bulkie roll

Tabasco sauce or ketchup (optional)

Makes 1 sandwich

The first time my sister-in-law went on a trip alone and left her kids overnight with her husband, he took them to McDonald's. Her three-year-old was astonished when a Happy Meal appeared at the drive-up window. "Dad," he exclaimed, "I didn't know the bank served food!"

Don't go there. This is so easy. It can be gussied up, but why fix what ain't broke?

. . . .

HOW TO MAKE

1 Cook the bacon in a small skillet according to the package directions and keep warm.

2 Heat the butter in a small nonstick skillet over medium heat. Crack the egg into a shallow bowl, then slide it into the pan. Season with salt and pepper. When it sets, flip the egg, top with the cheese, and cook the other side.

3 While you're cooking the egg, toast the English muffin or open up the bulkie roll, butterfly fashion. Slide the egg onto the bread. Maybe add a few shakes of Tabasco sauce or ketchup.

EGG SALAD SANDWICH

- 4 hard-boiled eggs (see page 39), peeled
- ¼ cup mayonnaise
- 1 celery stalk, strings removed, diced
- ½ small yellow onion, minced
- ½ red bell pepper, finely diced
- 2 teaspoons Dijon mustard
- Salt and freshly ground black pepper
- 4 slices whole-grain bread
- Lettuce

Makes 2 sandwiches

This high-protein, low-carb salad has gotten a bad rap because of gloppy deli versions served on soggy bread. But, oh, how wonderful an egg salad can be when well made, with its bright yellow yolk, flecks of herbs, and a bit of mayonnaise as the tie that binds. This basic salad can be embellished with many flavorings — crumbly bacon, a chopped pickle, diced red bell pepper, capers, olives, chives, dill, or a sprinkling of curry powder. Serve with lettuce, and maybe cheese and tomato, on hearty bread sliced on the thin side. Toasting the bread will help prevent sogginess.

HOW TO MAKE

1 Coarsely chop the eggs or lightly mash them in a medium bowl. Add the mayonnaise and blend. Add the celery, onion, bell pepper, mustard, and salt and pepper to taste.

2 Toast the bread, place some lettuce on two slices, top with the egg salad, and then top with the remaining two slices of bread. Serve immediately.

EGG SALAD, TAKE TWO

Isabel loves pickles and olives. For lunch I'll make her an egg salad sandwich and satisfy her craving by chopping pickles or olives into the filling and serving pickles on the side, too.

● ●

INGREDIENTS

3 hard-boiled eggs (see page 39), peeled

15 pimiento-stuffed green olives, coarsely chopped

3 tablespoons mayonnaise

1 teaspoon Dijon mustard

1 tablespoon minced fresh flat-leaf parsley

1 teaspoon minced onion

Salt and freshly ground black or white pepper

Makes 2 sandwiches

HOW TO MAKE

Coarsely chop the eggs or lightly mash them in a medium bowl. Add the olives, mayonnaise, mustard, parsley, onion, and salt and pepper to taste, and blend.

"O breakfast! O breakfast! The meal of my heart!
Bring porridge, bring sausage, bring fish for a start,
Bring kidneys and mushrooms and partridges' legs,
But let the foundation be bacon and eggs."

— Sir A. P. Herbert

Nom de Plume or Nom de Feather?

Naming our earliest chicks was a treat. The first batch we named with great care, the process being the topic of many dinner conversations. Do you go with quirky old-fashioned names such as Harriet, Gertrude, and Marge or fanciful ones like Moon Pie and Lulu or, as my father suggested, let loose with the puns: Fowler D. Nest, Henrietta, Coquette, Egglesby, Peck and Peck for twins, and Sarah Barnheart? A friend's mother kept a feisty little bantam rooster on her farm in Maine that she named Voldemort because he had all the appropriate personality traits. A hawk got him in the end, but while he was alive, for well over 5 years, he was a champion cock-a-doodle-doer. He rarely went more than a few minutes without issuing his call. They estimated conservatively that he crowed at least 100 times a day, every day, for his entire life. That's about 3,000 crows each month . . . or 36,000 a year . . . at least 180,000 in all.

The funny thing about naming chickens, however, is that the novelty wears off. Over the years, after we'd lost a few chickens, we became less enthusiastic about naming them. Trainer pinpointed it: It got harder to name them because a name brought focus to our sorrow when we lost one. Our most recent batch is so cute, however, that Isabel named them: Cheddar, Ham, Egg, Mango, and Ovo.

GREEK LEMON-CHICKEN SOUP

INGREDIENTS

6 cups chicken broth

⅓ cup Arborio rice

1 carrot, shredded

1 celery stalk, diced small

1 small yellow onion, chopped

2 sprigs fresh thyme

⅓ cup diced cooked chicken

2 eggs

2 egg yolks

¼ cup lemon juice

Salt and freshly ground black pepper

Lemon slices

Fresh flat-leaf parsley

Serves 4

This chicken and rice soup is a wholesome way to use up leftover roasted chicken. I like to serve it with pita toasts — I'll cut pita breads open and lay them butterflied on a baking sheet, butter the insides, sprinkle with herbs, and broil until golden brown (just a few minutes).

● ●

HOW TO MAKE

1 Combine the broth, rice, carrot, celery, onion, and thyme in a large soup pot. Bring to a boil, then reduce the heat and simmer until the rice is almost cooked, about 20 minutes. Add the chicken.

2 Beat the eggs, egg yolks, and lemon juice in a small bowl. Ladle 2 cups of the soup broth into a 1-quart measuring cup with a pouring spout. Slowly whisk in the egg mixture and then pour the broth and eggs back into the pot. Simmer, stirring often, until the rice is fully cooked and the chicken is warmed through, 5 to 10 minutes. Season with salt and pepper. Ladle into bowls and garnish with the lemon slices and parsley.

HOT & SOUR EGG DROP SOUP

INGREDIENTS

  6 cups chicken broth

  2 carrots, sliced

  1 bunch scallions, white part chopped, greens chopped and reserved for garnish

  4 tablespoons coarsely chopped black fungus mushrooms

3–4 tablespoons rice wine vinegar

  2 tablespoons soy sauce

  2 teaspoons freshly ground black pepper

  1 teaspoon minced fresh gingerroot

  ½ teaspoon cayenne pepper

  2 tablespoons cold water

  2 tablespoons cornstarch

  2 eggs, beaten

  1 can (6 oz.) sliced bamboo shoots, drained

1½ cups chopped firm tofu

Serves 4–6

Once called "the cement that holds the castle of cuisine together," eggs can bind, leaven, emulsify, clarify, and thicken other ingredients. They can add volume, moisture, and tenderness (sounds like Dolly Parton). If you are thickening a soup, add them just before serving, making sure the liquid isn't too hot, to prevent curdling. You could also temper the yolks first by adding them to a cup of the liquid that is slightly cooler, then pouring it into the larger pot.

. . . .

HOW TO MAKE

1 Combine the broth, carrots, scallions, mushrooms, vinegar, soy sauce, black pepper, gingerroot, and cayenne in a soup pot and bring to a boil. Reduce the heat and simmer for 5 minutes.

2 In a small bowl, mix the water with the cornstarch until dissolved, then slowly stir the mixture into the hot soup. Taste and adjust the hot and sour seasonings (rice wine vinegar, cayenne, gingerroot, black pepper), if necessary. Slowly pour in the eggs and stir clockwise to create silky strands. Add the bamboo shoots and tofu and cook briefly to warm. Remove from the heat and serve immediately, garnished with the green part of the scallions.

POACHED EGGS IN CHILE BROTH

This dish (*huevos en rabo de mestiza*) is a typical Mexican breakfast, though I serve it for lunch, too. Either way, warm flour tortillas are a good accompaniment.

INGREDIENTS

- 1 (16-ounce) can fire-roasted crushed tomatoes
- 3 cups chicken stock
- 2 tablespoons extra-virgin olive oil
- 1 medium yellow onion, julienned
- 1 teaspoon salt
- 1 teaspoon freshly ground black pepper
- 2 garlic cloves, minced
- 1 (7½-ounce) jar roasted red peppers, chopped
- 1 (7-ounce) can green chiles, chopped
- 8 eggs
- ½ cup shredded manchego cheese
- ⅓ cup sour cream

Serves 4–8

HOW TO MAKE

1 Combine the crushed tomatoes and 1 cup of the stock in a bowl.

2 Heat the olive oil in a large skillet over medium-high heat and sauté the onion with the salt and pepper until golden, about 10 minutes. Add the garlic and sauté for 1 minute longer. Add the roasted peppers, green chiles, tomato-broth mixture, and the remaining 2 cups of stock. Bring to a boil, then simmer for 5 minutes.

3 Gently crack the eggs into the simmering broth (some people crack them into a cup and slide them into the broth). Cook for 6 to 8 minutes, depending on how well done you like the yolk (I like it pretty well done in this dish), basting occasionally with the broth.

4 With a slotted spoon, scoop out the eggs and place one or two in each soup bowl. Ladle the broth over the eggs, garnish with the cheese and a spoonful of sour cream, and serve.

BRAZILIAN FISH STEW

INGREDIENTS

- 3 tablespoons palm oil (authentic) or extra-virgin olive oil (substitute)
- 1 large yellow onion, chopped
- ¼ cup lime juice
- 2 large tomatoes, peeled (optional) and chopped
- 1 red serrano chile, seeded and minced
- 1 garlic clove, chopped
- 3 tablespoons chopped fresh cilantro
-   Salt
- 3 pounds fleshy, firm white fish fillets, cut into 2-inch pieces
- ½ cup coconut milk
-   Cooked white or basmati rice
- 4 hard-boiled eggs (see page 39), peeled and sliced
-   Lime wedges

Serves 6

Note: In place of 3 pounds of fish, you could use 2 pounds of fish and 1 pound of mixed shellfish (clams, mussels, and shrimp).

Most cultures have a signature coastal fish stew — New England clam chowder, Puerto Rican *asopao*, bouillabaisse from Marseille — and Brazil, with its *moqueca* ("fish stew" in Portuguese), is no exception. This dish is traditionally served with white rice.

• •

HOW TO MAKE

1 Heat 1 tablespoon of the oil in a medium skillet over medium heat and sauté the onion until soft, about 10 minutes.

2 In a blender, purée the lime juice, tomatoes, chile, onion, garlic, 2 tablespoons of the cilantro, and salt to taste. Put the fish in a bowl, pour the purée over it, and let marinate for 1 hour.

3 Transfer the fish and marinade to a saucepan, add the coconut milk and the remaining 2 tablespoons of oil, cover, and simmer until the fish is cooked, 7 to 8 minutes. Serve over rice, garnished with egg slices, the remaining cilantro, and lime wedges on the side.

SALAD LYONNAISE

While this traditional French bistro salad is made with a poached egg on top of a bed of frisée, you can also mix frisée with other bitter greens and a bit of radicchio. It's a standard at Pastis, a popular French bistro in Manhattan's Meatpacking District.

INGREDIENTS

4 slices bacon

3 tablespoons extra-virgin olive oil

1½ tablespoons red wine vinegar

1 teaspoon Dijon mustard

2 handfuls frisée lettuce, torn into bite-size pieces

1 tablespoon minced shallot

Salt and freshly ground black pepper

2 poached eggs (see page 41), kept warm

¾ cup fresh croutons made from French bread (see Note)

Serves 2

Note: To make croutons, cut French bread into cubes, then toss with a little extra-virgin olive oil and garlic over medium heat in a skillet until browned on all sides.

HOW TO MAKE

1 Fry the bacon in a skillet until crisp, then remove and drain on paper towels, reserving 1 tablespoon of bacon fat in the skillet. Add the olive oil to the pan and heat, then whisk in the vinegar and mustard. When the bacon is cool, crumble it and leave on the paper towel.

2 Combine the frisée and shallot in a medium salad bowl, spoon in the warm dressing, and toss. Season with salt and pepper to taste. Divide the greens between two plates. Top with an egg, some bacon, and the croutons.

SAUSAGE BREAD PUDDING WITH SHIITAKES

INGREDIENTS

4 eggs

1 cup 2% milk

2 tablespoons Dijon mustard

1 tablespoon minced fresh basil

1 tablespoon chopped fresh flat-leaf parsley

¼ teaspoon freshly ground black pepper

2 links Italian turkey sausage (casings removed)

½ cup chopped red bell pepper

½ cup chopped shiitake mushrooms

½ cup chopped yellow onion

4 cups Italian bread, cut into 1-inch cubes (about 8 ounces or 4–6 slices)

2 plum tomatoes, thinly sliced

½ cup freshly grated Parmesan cheese

Serves 4

Note: You may do all the prep and then refrigerate the pie plate for up to 4 hours before baking the bread pudding.

I was introduced to shiitakes in the 1980s by my late first husband. Living on Manhattan's Upper East Side, Peter startled me one day by saying he wanted to buy a mushroom farm in the Berkshires with a friend from kindergarten. This was out of the box; Peter was a shipbroker, a Harvard Fly Club guy, with a degree in economics. While I'd had a hankering for a garden, my idea of the country was Katonah, not Green Acres. Yet never say never. We moved, and Peter and Bill became the first growers of fresh shiitakes in the United States. I became the volunteer cook and bottle washer, grilling shiitakes at food shows when I wasn't writing books on nuclear power and the unified field theory. It led me in wonderful new directions, and in some ways, it was my introduction to the food world.

. . . .

HOW TO MAKE

1 Preheat the oven to 375°F. Grease a 9-inch pie plate.

2 Whisk the eggs and milk in a medium bowl, then whisk in the mustard, basil, parsley, and black pepper. Crumble and cook the sausage in a skillet over medium heat until no longer pink. Add the bell pepper, mushrooms, and onion and cook until tender, about 10 minutes, then let cool.

3 Toss the bread with the vegetable mixture, then add the egg mixture and toss well to coat. Transfer to the pie plate, push down to compact, and layer the tomatoes around the edge, making a ring. Cover with foil and bake 40 to 45 minutes, until the custard has set. Uncover, sprinkle with the Parmesan, and continue baking 15 to 20 minutes longer, until puffed and golden on top. Let cool for 15 minutes before serving.

Biorecyclers

Hens are consummate recyclers and help you create
an extremely satisfying mini recycling program:
you feed them your leftover pizza crusts, pasta, and
eggshells, and in return they give you breakfast . . .
lunch . . . and dinner. After we started raising chickens,
we spent a week at a beach house and were appalled
by the amount of household food waste we were
throwing into the garbage. A chicken will eat its
weight in food every month, up to 9 pounds, so at
home we keep a pot on the stove and toss most of our
scraps into it, which, along with chicken feed, we feed
to them daily to ensure a balanced diet. The fact that
much of our scraps are organic is an added benefit to
both them and us when they "recycle" it into eggs.

Even a half-dozen hens will take care of most of your
biodegradable trash, helping to reduce landfills.
Indeed, the city of Diest, Belgium, gave 2,000 house-
holds three hens each in an effort to recycle more
biodegradable garbage and reduce the city's waste
management expenses. Chickens will also eat pesky
bugs, including ticks, and their waste provides nutritious compost for the soil in your garden.

One note on the scraps: Don't feed them anything
fibrous, like artichokes or celery. Some people also
contend that giving them fruit will stop egg production,
which we've never experienced. When you feed your
hens eggshells, which are a good source of calcium,
be sure to crush them up to sufficiently disguise them;
if they realize what they are eating and how good it
tastes, you may never see an egg in the coop again.

CROQUE MADAME

INGREDIENTS

Butter

8 slices bread (thicker is better)

8 slices Emmantaler cheese plus ¼ cup shredded

4 slices top-quality ham

4 eggs

Salt and freshly ground black pepper

Makes 4 sandwiches

Cecilia Hirsch is an incredible woman. She's the every-woman in a community — the friend you count on to run the clothing sale, head the PTO, volunteer when no one else is available, take a walk with, or share a pot of tea. She's also a photographer and college professor, but those are on a back burner while she raises her bilingual brood of four, speaking to them only in French so they are adept when they return to France to visit relatives. A natural cook with a deft hand, she gave me this recipe, in which a fried egg becomes the garnish that turns a Monsieur into a Madame. Serve this classic French café dish with crudités or salad.

HOW TO MAKE

1 Butter the slices of bread on one side. Layer the inside of each sandwich with 1 slice of cheese, then 1 slice of ham, then another slice of cheese. Put on a buttered baking sheet and place in warm oven on low broil to cook until cheese and ham are one and the bread is golden.

2 Meanwhile, heat butter in a large skillet and break the eggs into the pan, without letting the whites touch. Cook until set to your liking, then sprinkle with salt and pepper and add the ¼ cup of shredded Emmantaler cheese. To serve, use a spatula to slide an egg on top of each grilled sandwich.

Variations: Try goat cheese, or make a hole in the top bread layer and break the egg into it to cook directly on the cheese and ham, or add Dijon mustard to the inside of the sandwich before cooking.

Note: Emmantaler is in the Swiss cheese family.

SPAGHETTI ALLA CARBONARA

- 1 tablespoon extra-virgin olive oil
- 8 ounces thickly sliced pancetta or bacon, cut into small cubes
- 4 eggs
- ½ cup freshly grated Parmesan or pecorino cheese, plus extra for sprinkling
- 12 ounces spaghetti

  Salt and freshly ground black pepper

  Serves 6

We all need one of these in our back pocket: the perfect desperation dinner when the pantry is pretty bare. The heat of the pasta cooks the eggs to form a light custardy sauce. Pancetta, a seasoned Italian rolled meat similar to bacon, can be found in most supermarkets, but you can substitute thick-cut bacon.

HOW TO MAKE

1 Bring a large pot of salted water to a boil for the spaghetti.

2 Heat the olive oil in a large skillet over medium heat. Sauté the pancetta until crisp, about 10 minutes. Remove from the heat and pour off all but 2 tablespoons of fat. If necessary, add 1 or 2 tablespoons of water to the skillet and scrape up any bits that have stuck to the pan. Lightly beat the eggs and Parmesan in a bowl.

3 Cook the spaghetti in the boiling water according to the package directions. Reserve ⅓ cup of the cooking water before draining. Add the pasta to the skillet and toss with the pancetta and drippings. Add 2 to 4 tablespoons of the reserved pasta water to lightly coat the bottom of the skillet.

4 Remove the skillet from the heat and add the egg mixture, tossing continually until the pasta is lightly coated. If dry, add reserved water, 1 tablespoon at a time, until the eggs coat the pasta in a smooth sauce. Season with salt and lots of pepper. Transfer the pasta to a large serving bowl and sprinkle with more grated Parmesan.

CHILES RELLENOS

1½ pounds fresh poblano chiles (or substitute Anaheim or New Mexico chiles)

1¾ cups shredded cheddar or Mexican blend cheese

3 eggs

⅔ cup whole milk

¼ cup unbleached all-purpose flour

½ teaspoon salt

Freshly ground black pepper

Serves 6–8

When Christopher Columbus landed in the West Indies, he called the green chile plants "peppers," thinking that black pepper was related to the chile plant, and thus beginning a nomenclature confusion that persists to this day. Chiles rellenos ("stuffed chiles") is a Mexican dish from the Puebla region in which roasted poblano chiles are stuffed with cheese and baked in a light custard. Serve them with salsa or sour cream.

. . . .

HOW TO MAKE

1 Preheat the broiler and line a baking sheet with aluminum foil.

2 Arrange the chiles in a single layer on the baking sheet and broil until they are charred on all sides, turning once or twice for even cooking. Wrap the chiles in the foil and let sit for 10 to 15 minutes to steam. Remove the charred skin and stems (don't rinse them), split in half lengthwise, and scrape out the seeds. Pat dry.

3 Lower the oven temperature to 350°F. Lightly grease an 8-inch square baking dish. Place a layer of chiles evenly in the bottom of the dish. Sprinkle with 1 cup of the cheese. Top with the remaining chile halves.

4 Beat the eggs, milk, flour, salt, and pepper in a blender or bowl. Pour over the top of the chiles. Sprinkle with the remaining ¾ cup of cheese. Cover with foil and bake for 25 to 30 minutes. Remove the foil and bake for 5 to 10 minutes longer or until just set. Let rest for 5 minutes before serving.

WILD MUSHROOM RAGOUT WITH POACHED EGGS

3–4 tablespoons extra-virgin olive oil

4–5 ramps or scallions (white and green parts), sliced

2 garlic cloves, thinly sliced

2 cups fresh wild mushrooms, using whatever is best available (morels, chanterelles, and hen of the woods are excellent, but you can also use shiitakes and oyster mushrooms), cleaned, stems discarded, and sliced

2 cups chicken stock

1 cup dry white wine

1 tablespoon fresh thyme

Crunchy sea salt and freshly ground black pepper

1 tablespoon white vinegar

6 eggs

Truffle oil

Finely chopped fresh chives

Serves 6

Hans Morris is one of those amazing guys who seem accomplished at everything they tackle. Commanding in the world of finance, he's also a closet rock 'n' roller with a deep-seated knowledge of the music scene, equally at home below 14th Street as on the Upper East Side. He also loves to cook; when invited to his house for dinner, I'll bring him eggs from our hens, and he'll shoot me an e-mail the following day saying that he whipped up the eggs into something like "Tajine of Ducks' Tongues with Hundred Year–Style Eggs." He served this exquisite ragout to us on one visit, mentioning that it is particularly delicious in the spring when fresh ramps and morels are available. He probably forages for them himself.

. . . .

HOW TO MAKE

1 Heat the olive oil in a large skillet over medium heat. Add the ramps and garlic and sauté until soft, about 5 minutes. Add the mushrooms and sauté until soft, 15 minutes or so. Add the stock, wine, thyme, and salt and pepper to taste. Simmer for 30 minutes over low heat.

2 Just before serving, heat enough water to cover the eggs in a skillet large enough to hold all the eggs. Add the vinegar. When the water is boiling, crack each egg individually and gently add one at a time to the skillet. Cover, turn off the heat, and let cook for 3½ minutes. Do not overcook.

3 While the eggs are cooking, spoon the ragout into individual serving bowls. Scoop out the eggs with a slotted spoon and nestle one into each serving of ragout. Then drizzle each egg with a little truffle oil and sprinkle with sea salt, black pepper, and a few chives. Serve immediately.

CRÈME D'EPINARDS AU GRATIN
(Baked Spinach Gratin)

INGREDIENTS

- 10 ounces fresh spinach
- 1 egg
- 1¼ cups heavy cream (see Note)
- Freshly grated nutmeg
- Salt and freshly ground black or white pepper
- ½ cup freshly grated Parmesan cheese
- ½ cup shredded gruyère cheese (2 ounces)
- 1 tablespoon butter

Serves 6–8

Note: If you prefer a more custardy dish, use 2 eggs and 2 cups of cream. You may also top this with bread-crumbs before baking if you like.

My husband's aunt Verna is a great cook. She hails from Helotes, Texas, where years ago she had a neighbor named Sparky Boxall, who had trained at Le Cordon Bleu in Paris and later taught culinary classes for years in Washington, D.C. Sparky was a live wire, serving the neighborhood kids beef tongue and tonic water (never soda) and giving them cooking classes on their birthdays. She gave Verna lessons, and the two eventually offered classes at home. This dish was developed by Verna and Sparky, and it's ideal to serve at a dinner party.

HOW TO MAKE

1 Wash and stem the spinach. Toss into a large pot with the water still clinging to the leaves. Do not add any more water. Cover and cook over medium heat, tossing with a fork from time to time. As soon as the spinach has begun to wilt, 2 to 3 minutes, transfer to a sieve and drain. Press lightly with a fork to remove some of the moisture, then finely chop on a cutting board. The amount will look extremely small and cause your heart to skip a beat. Do not fret.

2 Preheat the oven to 400°F.

3 Beat the egg in a medium bowl. Add the cream, nutmeg, and salt and pepper to taste, and stir in the chopped spinach and ¼ cup each of the Parmesan and gruyère. Blend well. You may make it up to this point the day before and refrigerate until 1 hour before baking.

4 Butter a 6- by 10-inch shallow baking dish, preferably ceramic. Pour the mixture into the dish and sprinkle the top with the remaining ¼ cup each of the Parmesan and the gruyère. Dot with the butter and bake for 25 minutes, or until golden and slightly puffed. Serve at once from the dish.

🍃 Oh Gratin

A classic gratin consists of a previously cooked vegetable that is chopped, sliced, or
puréed; mixed with a light custard base of eggs and milk or cream; well seasoned; and
topped with grated cheese or breadcrumbs, or both. It is then baked until the custard is
set and the top a beautiful golden brown, and it is served directly from the baking dish.
Neither creamed nor souffléd, it is really a quiche baked in a dish instead of a pastry
case. Somewhat heavier than a quiche, it characteristically uses a larger amount of
vegetables, less milk or cream, and fewer eggs.

Broccoli, cauliflower, onions, potatoes, spinach, and zucchini make a delicious gratin
in any combination, and all can be prepared the day before and refrigerated in a
bowl. Just give them a final stir to blend well before baking. These dishes require
little attention while baking and go straight to the table. All are excellent with grilled
or roasted meats of any kind, and with lightly sauced veal or chicken, or served as a
luncheon entrée with a salad.

CHALLAH BREAD

This recipe, which makes a tender, sweet loaf, was given to me by my friend and Williamstown neighbor Darra Goldstein, who is editor in chief of the food journal *Gastronomica: The Journal of Food and Culture*. It was given to her many years ago, when she was in graduate school, and she's been making it ever since.

INGREDIENTS

2 packages active dry yeast

2 cups warm water (105–115°F)

1¼ cups vegetable oil

½ cup sugar

4 teaspoons salt

3 eggs, beaten

7 cups unbleached all-purpose flour

Makes 3 loaves

HOW TO MAKE

1 Dissolve the yeast in the warm water in a large bowl. Stir in the oil, sugar, salt, and beaten eggs, reserving just enough of the eggs to brush onto the loaves before baking. Stir in half of the flour, then mix in enough of the remaining flour to make a soft, pliable dough.

2 Turn out the dough onto a floured surface and knead until smooth and springy, about 8 minutes. Place in a greased bowl, turning to grease the top of the dough, cover, and leave to rise until doubled, about 1½ hours.

3 Grease three baking sheets. Separate the dough into three equal pieces. Working with one piece at a time, divide the dough in thirds. With your hands, roll each third into a strand about 12 inches long and arrange them on a work surface pointing toward you. Pinch the three strands together at the far end, then braid the loaves, working toward you. Pinch the bottom ends of the strands together to seal, and place the loaf on a prepared baking sheet. Repeat the braiding process with the other two pieces of dough.

4 Preheat the oven to 350°F.

5 Let the loaves rise until slightly puffy, about 30 minutes. Gently brush the loaves with the reserved beaten egg, then bake for about 1 hour, until nicely brown on top.

Chickens in the New World

Over the years, some historians assumed that Christopher Columbus introduced chickens to the New World on his second expedition, in 1493. Unlike his first exploratory trek, the purpose of his second expedition was to colonize, and in Columbus's flotilla of 17 ships that landed first in Puerto Rico and then Hispaniola, he brought almost 1,500 settlers and livestock, including horses, sheep, cattle, and chickens.

Many people believe that the Araucana chicken, a desirable heirloom breed that lays bluish green eggs, is a direct descendent of hens that the Spanish conquistadores brought to South America, but recent findings suggest that chickens may have beaten Columbus to the New World. Radiocarbon dating and ancient DNA sequencing from a chicken bone found at an archaeological site on the Arauco Peninsula in Chile indicated the chicken not only dated back to 1321–1407, but also had a shared DNA sequencing with Polynesian chickens, which have been in the Pacific for 3,000 years. That ruffled some feathers.

FRESH QUIET EGGS

EGG-cess

"It may be the cock that crows, but it is the hen that lays the eggs."

— Margaret Thatcher

Once our girls started laying, we soon had too many eggs. Our rule became that if there were a dozen eggs in the refrigerator, Trainer could sell the rest. They were gorgeous — with colors ranging from light brown to blue — and he priced them $2 cheaper than our local health food store and our CSA farm.

He made a sandwich board, set up a card table, and tried selling them at the foot of our driveway with a poetic roadside sign advertising "Fresh quiet eggs." It was a total bust (we live on a busy road), so he tried selling them on a friend's front lawn (also a total bust; people don't buy food from strangers, other than lemonade). Then he cooked up the idea of "eggmails," which were a hit. When he has a dozen eggs to sell, he sends out an e-mail to his customers — neighbors, teachers, our museum colleagues, and people interested in fresh eggs — and it's a race to see who gets the fresh eggs first.

His eggmails are hilarious. On election night he offered a victory discount; he runs contests; he embeds hidden text in his e-mails so that only those who get the clue know to buy the eggs; and sometimes he simply sends a long e-mail that cryptically reads "egggggggs." (This cookbook cut down on his egg sales substantially while I was testing and retesting many recipes, but I imagine he'll start selling copies of the book along with the eggs when it's published.)

When his younger sister, Isabel, on whom he pawns off chicken chores as often as he can, decided she wanted to get into the act, he raised the price of eggs from $3 to $3.50 (explaining to his customers that his six-year-old sister had to get a cut), and gave her 50 cents as long as she helped with the chores. Now eight years old, she no longer helps much; she decided shoe shining was more lucrative, as her father gives her $2 per shine.

Selling eggs is an age-old childhood business. Back in the 1930s, Richard Aplin, the father of a friend of mine, sold eggs to the neighbors when he was living in Waban, Massachusetts. Richard's grandfather, who had a dairy farm in Vermont, would send him a dozen pullets every September. Resourceful at the age of 13, he had a label printed up ("Aplin's Best Eggs, from contented hens"). It was his job to take care of the New Hampshire Reds, clean the chicken house, and pocket the profits. He eventually became a professor of agricultural economics at Cornell University, and when asked recently about chickens, Richard said without hesitation, "I hate chickens." He allowed that he enjoyed the fact that his hens had personalities and he could tell them apart, but cleaning the coop was a terrible job. "Cows have much more personality than hens," he summed up. "I prefer milk to eggs." But that's another book.

So what can you do with all those eggs, besides sell them? You can throw them. We go to an old-fashioned dude ranch in Wyoming, and one of the most anticipated events of the visit is the egg-throwing contest, in which partners ages 5 to 80 endeavor to toss an egg 20 feet or more between them. Egg-tossing games have been associated with Easter since medieval times, a lingering symbol of rebirth from pagan times. An egg will become addled if left unrefrigerated too long, and in days of old it was common for people to throw rotten eggs to express their displeasure at plays and parades. Indeed, when I crewed on boat deliveries from Maine to the British Virgin Islands, as we traveled down the Intracoastal Waterway it was an accepted custom to pelt eggs at a boat that sped too fast along the narrow channel and upset the boats in its wake.

Eggs also make great gifts. I have a collection of wicker baskets in my pantry that I've found at tag sales, and when we are invited to someone's house for dinner, instead of bringing wine, I take a dozen blue or brown eggs in a basket, nestled in a linen tea towel. I also pickle eggs to give as presents to my children's teachers.

And, of course, you can cook with your extra eggs. This chapter contains recipes that use an abundance of eggs, for those days when you're feeling plentiful and your throwing arm is bad.

EGG-CESS

PICKLED EGGS

INGREDIENTS

12 hard-boiled eggs (see
   page 39)

3 cups malt vinegar

1 cup water

1 small dried chile, split open

20 black peppercorns

2 (4-inch) cinnamon sticks

2 bay leaves

Makes 12 eggs

Pickling eggs in vinegar has been a preserving technique since the days before refrigeration. Decorate an attractive glass Ball jar with a ribbon and you've got a homemade gift. I always attach a card, too, explaining the ingredients and uses. Pickled eggs cut open, dusted with a bit of coarse salt, are delicious on picnics, served with cold cuts and potato salad, or laid out on an hors d'oeuvre board with gherkins, olives, cheeses, and crackers. When making pickled eggs, you can play with the seasonings to achieve various flavors.

HOW TO MAKE

1 Peel the eggs and pack them in a sterilized jar with an airtight lid, leaving an inch at the top for the liquid alone. Heat the vinegar, water, chile, peppercorns, cinnamon, and bay leaves in a saucepan until the liquid begins to boil. Reduce the heat and simmer for 10 minutes. Remove from the heat and allow to cool to room temperature.

2 Strain the liquid and pour it over the eggs in the jar, covering them completely by 1 inch. Seal the jar and store in the refrigerator for 2 weeks before eating.

Easter Eggs

Centuries ago in France, eggs were such a luxury that they were forbidden during Lent. It was not until Maundy Thursday and Good Friday that people would collect their eggs so that they might be blessed on Easter Sunday. In the north country where we live, when Easter arrives the snow is finally letting up, the sap is coursing through the veins of the maple trees, and spring, a perpetual sign of renewal, is in the air.

The word *Easter* is derived from Eostra, the ancient goddess of spring, dawn, and fertility. With Easter celebrated on the first Sunday following the first full moon past the vernal equinox, many Easter customs can be traced back to archaic rites of spring.

The egg is an ancient symbol of new life and fertility. Myths that have come down to us from many cultures view the egg as the source of life. Going into spring with newborn chicks is a great way to celebrate a season of new beginnings.

Devilish Twist

My mother-in-law Mary Jane is a natural cook; she'll cook something, save every leftover, and turn out a great concoction the next night, the leftovers completely disguised. She's also a marvelous babysitter, because she'll come in a minute to take care of our kids if we're thinking of going away. But she's not wild about the hens. "I don't do chickens," she'll announce, as she takes on the load of caring for two kids, a cat, and a gecko. But she likes the eggs.

Her recipe for spicy deviled eggs calls for cream cheese and sour cream, in equal parts, in place of mayonnaise. Add teaspoons of cream cheese and sour cream to the yolks until the consistency is soft and it mounds with a spoon. Add a bit of mustard and a fruit-based habanero hot sauce (for a dozen eggs, 1 or 2 teaspoons of hot sauce, or to taste). Then fold in some fresh chives and fill the egg white halves.

AUNT JUDITH'S DEVILED EGGS

INGREDIENTS

12 hard-boiled eggs (see page 39)

¼–½ cup mayonnaise

3 tablespoons Jump Up and Kiss Me Original Hot Sauce or other hot sauce with curry

3 tablespoons lemon juice

3 garlic cloves, crushed

Salt and freshly ground white pepper

Paprika

Sliced pimiento-stuffed olives (optional)

Makes 24 egg halves

Family parties with the Thompson clan in Oklahoma are fun affairs, with plenty of food and always deviled eggs, be it Christmas, a christening, Easter . . . basically any time there's a get-together. I asked the Thompson ladies to give me their particular deviled recipes, and this is Aunt Judith's. If you prepare it several hours ahead, cover the eggs loosely with plastic wrap to prevent moisture from accumulating.

· ·

HOW TO MAKE

1 Carefully peel the eggs and cut in half. Gently remove the yolks and place in a mixing bowl. Mash with a pastry blender as fine as possible. Add the mayonnaise 2 tablespoons at a time, continuing to mash and smooth the yolks, until you reach the desired consistency. It should be easily spreadable but still hold together. Add the hot sauce, lemon juice, garlic, and salt and pepper to taste.

2 Fill the egg white halves until gently heaped. Dust lightly with paprika. If you'd like, garnish with sliced stuffed olives.

CAJUN PICKLED EGGS

INGREDIENTS

12 hard-boiled eggs (see page 39)

2 cups white wine vinegar

1 cup water

2 red chiles, cut lengthwise, or 1 teaspoon red pepper flakes

2 tablespoons black or white peppercorns

1 teaspoon salt

1 teaspoon sugar

Makes 12 eggs

When we run out of pickles, my husband saves the juice in the jar and sticks hard-boiled eggs into it. Then he puts it back into the refrigerator and in a few weeks, voilà, we have pickled eggs. It falls a bit short as a cookbook recipe, but it's tasty and easy. This recipe takes a little longer, maybe 10 minutes. Adding water cuts the acidity and keeps the eggs from getting too rubbery. You can use any kind of vinegar and can experiment with the chiles — a mixture of red, green, and yellow is pretty, for example, or a combination of long skinny ones such as cayennes and short stubby ones such as serranos.

HOW TO MAKE

1 Peel the eggs and pack them in a sterilized jar with a lid, leaving an inch at the top for the liquid alone. Combine the vinegar, water, chiles, peppercorns, salt, and sugar in a saucepan, bring to a boil, and simmer for 10 minutes.

2 Allow the liquid to cool, then pour the brine over the eggs. Strain if you wish. Seal the jar and refrigerate for 2 weeks before eating.

VERNA'S STUFFED EGGS

INGREDIENTS

10 hard-boiled eggs
(see page 39)

10 ounces fresh spinach

⅓ cup freshly grated
Parmesan cheese

Salt and freshly ground
black pepper

Freshly grated nutmeg

¼ cup heavy cream, plus more
if needed

Makes 20 egg halves

Note: Ten ounces of fresh
spinach will yield ¾ cup of
cooked chopped spinach. If
the eggs are small, this may
be too much. There should be
enough spinach to give a good
green color but not so much
that it is overpowering. Start
by adding ½ cup to the yolk
mixture and taste and note
its appearance; if needed, you
can then add more.

My husband's aunt Verna, like many of the other
Thompson women of her generation, is confident, funny,
and formidable, both in and out of the kitchen. The
green color in these stuffed eggs makes them attractive as a Christmas dish, and because they should be
prepared the day before serving, they are a welcome
addition to a cocktail party menu. You can make this
dish in stages and assemble when ready.

HOW TO MAKE

1 Peel the eggs, cut in half lengthwise, and remove and
reserve the yolks.

2 Stem and wash the spinach. Put it in a large pot with the
water still clinging to the leaves. Place over high heat
without any additional water, cover, and cook, tossing with
a fork frequently. As soon as the spinach has wilted, 2 to
3 minutes, remove from the heat. Place the spinach in a
colander and drain well, pressing with a fork to extract
liquid. Then squeeze gently with your hands to extract
remaining liquid. Chop fine. The spinach may be prepared
a day in advance and stored, covered, in the refrigerator
until needed.

3 To assemble the dish, press the egg yolks through
a sieve into a medium bowl. Add the spinach and
Parmesan. Season with salt carefully, as Parmesan
tends to be salty, then add pepper and nutmeg to taste.
Add the cream and mix thoroughly with a fork. Taste
for seasoning and correct the consistency if desired by
adding more cream to make a soft, moist paste that is
neither crumbly nor soggy.

4 Stuff the egg white halves with this mixture, neatly
mounding the stuffing into a dome. Cover well with
plastic wrap and chill for 24 hours before serving.

OEUFS À L'AIL
(Eggs with Garlic-Anchovy Sauce)

INGREDIENTS

10–12 large garlic cloves, peeled

10–12 oil-packed anchovy fillets, well drained

2 tablespoons large capers

3 tablespoons olive oil

2 teaspoons white wine vinegar

Freshly ground black pepper

6 hard-boiled eggs (see page 39)

Serves 8–10

Variation: Like most other old Provençal dishes, this has several versions. For example, you might halve the eggs lengthwise, remove the yolks, and add them to the mortar along with the garlic, anchovies, and capers. Pound everything together, add the oil very slowly, and then add the vinegar. Season with pepper. The resulting sauce will be thicker due to the yolks. Fill the whites with this mixture, arrange the eggs on a serving dish, and refrigerate. If you try this version, use 8 eggs rather than 6.

Oeufs à l'Ail is a title that is both misleading and something of an understatement. This rustic dish from the late Sparky Boxall is related to a family of hors d'oeuvres derived from a pungent Provençal preparation known as *anchoïade*. An *anchoïade* is a sauce, or paste, involving anchovies as the principal ingredient. It is served with many foods, both raw and cooked. "It has a great deal of character and is not likely to appeal to the less adventuresome diner," says Joe's aunt Verna wryly. "It will prove disastrous to palates that have not cultivated a taste for anchovies. However, it provides an element of surprise and interest to an array of hors d'oeuvres, or to a buffet, and it blends admirably with any combination." It is easily and quickly prepared.

HOW TO MAKE

1 Put the garlic cloves in a small saucepan. Cover with cold water and bring to a boil. Gently cook over medium heat for 10 minutes. Drain and cool. Put the cloves in a mortar and pound with a pestle to crush them. Add the anchovies and capers and pound with the pestle to a smooth paste. Add the oil almost drop by drop, stirring continuously to make a smooth sauce. Add the vinegar, stirring slowly. Then add the pepper to taste.

2 Spread the sauce (it will be rather sparse) in a shallow serving dish to cover the bottom. Peel the eggs, slice them thick, and arrange over the sauce in overlapping rows. Chill and serve.

Grade A™
Egg Scale

🐔 Lost Chicks

Every year we survey our flock in February and purchase more chicks around Easter if we're getting low. A few years ago we ordered some chicks through the mail, and they didn't come on the day they were supposed to. I called, and the woman said don't worry. I called the next day, and the woman still said don't worry. I called the third day, and she told me that they'd been delivered to Jennifer Thompson in Ohio. Only problem is: I live in Massachusetts. We were all so sad to think of those poor chicks, hoping that Jennifer Thompson in Ohio had been home pleasantly surprised by the Easter gift bestowed upon her.

CAVIAR EGGS

INGREDIENTS

6 hard-boiled eggs (see page 39)

2–3 tablespoons mayonnaise or sour cream or a combination

1 tablespoon minced white onion, scallion, or chives

Salt and freshly ground black pepper

6 tablespoons large-grain caviar

12 small dill or flat-leaf parsley sprigs (optional)

Makes 12 egg halves

Years ago, when the food writer John Hadamuscin orchestrated a series of food photo shoots at my house for a cookbook he was writing, we had a lot of fun, and I appreciated his entertaining style, which was broad, slightly indulgent, and decorative. He went on to write about holiday entertaining, and this recipe is taken loosely from one of his. Pairing caviar with eggs is a natural in terms of texture, color, and flavor.

HOW TO MAKE

1 Peel the eggs and cut them in half lengthwise. Scoop out the yolks and mix in a bowl with the mayonnaise and onion until smooth. Season with salt and pepper to taste, remembering that the caviar is salty. Transfer to a pastry bag and pipe into the halved egg whites, or (if you don't have a pastry bag) mound the filling gently into the egg whites.

2 Just before serving, scoop a bit of caviar on top of each egg (you can have fun with the caviar colors) and decorate each half with a sprig of dill.

CHEESE STRATA

INGREDIENTS

Butter

12 slices white, wheat, or French bread

12 ounces sharp cheddar cheese, sliced

1½ cups cooked broccoli

2 cups diced cooked chicken or ham

6 eggs, lightly beaten

3 cups milk

½ cup white wine

2 tablespoons minced onion

1 teaspoon dry mustard

½ teaspoon salt

Pinch of cayenne pepper

Freshly grated nutmeg

1 cup shredded cheddar cheese (4 ounces)

Serves 12

My mother-in-law, Mary Jane, is a formidable cook, blending no-nonsense, down-home Oklahoma cooking with a sophisticated palate and a deft touch. She can turn out a beautiful meal from the most meager leftovers, and it's always a treat to go to her house, because you know the hospitality will be plentiful and the food very good. The Thompsons are a big gang — six brothers in my father-in-law Jim's generation — and when they get together, which is often, the sisters-in-law cook copious amounts of food. It's high time our generation took over the work, but none of us is as good, and we'd miss their cooking too much. Mary Jane serves this old-fashioned breakfast casserole on Christmas morning with fruit salad.

. . . .

HOW TO MAKE

1 Butter a 9- by 13-inch baking dish. Cut 12 doughnuts and holes from the bread using a doughnut cutter (you can also use an inverted glass to cut circles). Lay the remaining scraps of bread in the bottom of the dish. Place the cheddar in a layer over the bread, add a layer of broccoli, then add the chicken. Arrange the bread doughnuts and holes on top.

2 Combine the eggs, milk, wine, onion, dry mustard, salt, and cayenne in a bowl and pour over the bread. Grate a little nutmeg over the top, cover, and refrigerate overnight.

3 Preheat the oven to 325°F.

4 Remove the strata from the refrigerator 1 hour before baking. Bake, uncovered, for 2 hours. About 4 minutes before it's done, sprinkle with the shredded cheese and return to the oven. Let stand for 10 minutes before serving.

GRUYÈRE & BROCCOLI QUICHE

INGREDIENTS

Pastry for a 9-inch single-crust pie

1 tablespoon butter

¾ cup chopped yellow onions or scallions

1 cup broccoli or raw spinach, steamed

1½ cups cubed gruyère cheese (or cheddar, Monterey jack, or swiss)

4 eggs

2 cups milk or light cream

1 teaspoon dried thyme or oregano

Salt and freshly ground black pepper

Serves 6

Note: Chopped cooked bacon is tasty sprinkled in along with the broccoli.

The poor quiche has been much maligned, the word still equated with "wimp" in some circles, due to the runaway success in the early '80s of *Real Men Don't Eat Quiche*, a satire of male stereotyping and a kitschy call to male independence. Essentially a creamy egg and milk custard in a crusty open pie shell that can include (or not) any number of ingredients, quiche is one of the most versatile dishes. Serve it hot or cold and fill it with vegetables, meats, or whatever cheeses you have in the bin. Quiche is a keeper, as they say in my family, and shouldn't be underestimated. I guess we could call it an egg tart. After I make it, I'm going to go out and pump some iron.

. . . .

HOW TO MAKE

1 Preheat the oven to 375°F.

2 Line a 9-inch pie plate with the pastry and prick the bottom in several places with a fork to prevent bubbling. Bake for 5 minutes, then remove from the oven.

3 Heat the butter in a medium skillet and sauté the onions until soft and translucent, about 10 minutes. Spread the onions over the bottom of the pie shell. Layer the broccoli over the onions. Layer the cheese on top.

4 Whisk the eggs in a bowl with the milk, thyme, and salt and pepper to taste. Pour over the cheese. Bake for 35 minutes, or until a knife inserted into the center comes out clean. Let cool slightly before serving.

MJ'S EGG CASSEROLE

This brunch recipe is good freshly made, and it's even better if prepped the day before and refrigerated overnight before baking. My mother-in-law serves it with hot curried fruit, crisp asparagus, and croissants.

• •

INGREDIENTS

4 tablespoons butter

¼ cup unbleached all-purpose flour

1 cup cream

1 cup milk

2 cups shredded sharp cheddar or swiss cheese (8 ounces)

¼ cup chopped fresh flat-leaf parsley

¼ teaspoon dried marjoram

¼ teaspoon dried thyme

⅛ teaspoon garlic powder

Pinch of cayenne pepper

18 hard-boiled eggs (see page 39), thinly sliced

1 pound bacon, cooked, drained, and crumbled

Serves 6–8

HOW TO MAKE

1 Preheat the oven to 350°F and butter a 9- by 13-inch baking dish.

2 Make a cream sauce by melting the butter in a saucepan over medium heat and stirring in the flour until smooth. Lower heat and gradually add the cream, milk, and cheese and stir until melted. Add the parsley, marjoram, thyme, garlic powder, and cayenne.

3 Layer the egg slices, crumbled bacon, and sauce in the prepared dish, ending with the sauce. Cover and bake for 40 minutes. If making the night before, remove from the refrigerator 1 hour before you want to bake the casserole, and add 20 minutes to the baking time. Let it rest for 5 to 10 minutes before serving.

MEXICAN CASSEROLE

INGREDIENTS

10 eggs

½ cup unbleached all-purpose flour

1 teaspoon baking powder

1 pint small-curd cottage cheese

4 cups shredded Monterey jack cheese (1 pound)

4 tablespoons butter, melted

½ teaspoon salt

2 (4-ounce) cans green chiles, diced

Serves 6

When I married Joe, I married into the big Oklahoma Thompson clan. The Thompson women of his mother's generation love to cook and do it effortlessly, folding it into their conversation and parties as easily as they do the laughter and ribbing. When Joe and I got married, on a beautiful September afternoon in our New England backyard under an apple tree, they all showed up . . . early that morning. They wanted to check me out, as well as the china, the sterling flatware, the fixings, and the way I did things. They drove up the driveway, just to take a peek, and found me in shorts, sweating in a cloud of steam, ironing a mound of my great-grandmother's linen napkins. They came in and took over, cheerfully.

That night they gave us a Cuisinart food processor as a wedding gift, with the eldest aunt announcing dryly that the choice was either to pool their resources and give us a really nice wedding gift or to take a vacation and come to our wedding, and they all voted for the latter. This tasty casserole is from Aunt Judith.

HOW TO MAKE

1 Preheat the oven to 350°F. Butter a 9- by 13-inch baking dish.

2 Beat the eggs in a large bowl. Add the flour, baking powder, cottage cheese, jack cheese, butter, and salt and blend. Stir in the chiles. Spoon the mixture into the baking dish and bake for 35 minutes, or until set. Let rest for 5 to 10 minutes before serving.

🐔 Chicks and Kids

In terms of cleaning the coop, it's probably a universal fact that kids don't like to do it. Matter of fact, neither do I. Our deal with the kids is that they feed and water the birds, open up their coop in the morning, and close it every night. Trainer maintains the eggmail database and services the customers, though Joe or I often end up delivering the eggs. We buy the food and clean the coop twice yearly.

When querying friends whose families raise chickens about their kids' involvement, I've gotten responses ranging from laughter at the suggestion that their kids actually take care of the chickens to frankness about the fact that kids can easily feed and take care of the birds but often need reminding.

EGG FOO YONG

INGREDIENTS

½ cup chicken broth

1½ tablespoons oyster sauce

1 tablespoon hoisin sauce

1½ teaspoons soy sauce

1½ teaspoons rice wine vinegar

1½ teaspoons cornstarch

1 bunch scallions

8 eggs

1 teaspoon toasted sesame oil

¼ teaspoon salt

¼ teaspoon freshly ground black pepper

2 tablespoons canola oil

1 cup bean sprouts

1 teaspoon minced garlic

1 teaspoon grated fresh gingerroot

6 ounces large shrimp, peeled, cooked, and chopped

Serves 4

In *The Honeymooners,* Ed Norton claimed he could set his watch by the time it took for the smell of the egg foo yong from the neighboring Chinese restaurant to drift up to his apartment window. Although pooh-poohed in some culinary circles (too tiki, too tacky) and assumed to be a concoction found only in Chinese-American restaurants, there is evidence that this omelet is authentically Chinese, based on a Shanghai dish called *Fu Yong.* One of the few Chinese dishes in which the sauce is prepared separately and poured over it, this one lends itself to any number of fillings — not just bean sprouts and shrimp, but also beef, barbecued pork, broccoli, mushrooms, and tofu. If you prepare it with vegetables, blanch or stir-fry them before adding them to the egg mixture to bring out the flavor.

HOW TO MAKE

1 Whisk together the broth, oyster sauce, hoisin sauce, soy sauce, vinegar, and cornstarch in a small saucepan over medium heat. Bring to a simmer, whisking occasionally, and simmer for 2 minutes. Remove the sauce from the heat and set aside, keeping it warm.

2 Separate the white and green parts and then chop the scallions. Beat the eggs in a bowl with the sesame oil and the salt and pepper and set aside. Heat the canola oil in a nonstick skillet over medium heat and sauté the white parts of the scallions, the bean sprouts, garlic, and gingerroot for about 5 minutes. Add the shrimp and half the scallion greens, then pour in the eggs and cook, stirring occasionally, until the eggs are done but still a little loose. Cover the skillet and cook until eggs are set into a pancake, 3 to 4 minutes.

3 Divide the egg pancake among four plates, drizzle the sauce over the eggs, and top with the remaining scallion greens. Serve immediately.

VERNA'S CRÊPES AL PROSCIUTTO

This recipe is delightful at breakfast or brunch. If you don't have a crêpe pan, use a small cast-iron skillet. Asparagus, broccoli, or another vegetable may be substituted for the prosciutto. This recipe can also be prepared the day before; just bring it to room temperature before baking.

● ●

INGREDIENTS

For the Crêpes
5 eggs

2 tablespoons water

1 tablespoon butter

For the Filling
1 tablespoon butter

1 tablespoon plus 1 teaspoon unbleached all-purpose flour

¾ cup whole milk

Salt and freshly ground black pepper

2 slices prosciutto, chopped

For the Topping
½ cup heavy cream

¼ cup shredded cheese such as gruyère, gouda, Bel Paese, or fontina (1 ounce)

Serves 4

HOW TO MAKE

1 For the crêpes, beat the eggs and water in a medium bowl with a fork or a whisk. Melt some butter in the crêpe pan(s). It will take approximately 2½ tablespoons of the egg mixture for each (I use a ¼-cup measuring cup and do not fill to the top). Tip the pan to cover surface and cook quickly. Turn with a spatula and cook briefly on the second side. Turn out upside down onto a plate, and stack the crêpes as they're ready. You should have enough batter to make 8 crêpes.

2 Preheat the oven to 450°F and butter a shallow baking dish.

3 For the filling, melt the butter in a small skillet over medium heat and add the flour, whisking for a minute or so to make a light-colored roux. Add the milk and the salt and pepper to taste, and bring to a boil. Simmer for 3 to 4 minutes, then add the prosciutto and simmer for about a minute longer.

4 Put about 1 tablespoon of the filling on each crêpe, then roll up tight. Place close together in the prepared baking dish, seam-side down. To top, drizzle the cream over the crêpes, covering them, then sprinkle the cheese over the cream and crêpes. Bake for 10 to 14 minutes, or until the cheese has melted and is bubbly. Serve immediately.

POTATO & CORN FRITTATA

INGREDIENTS

3 tablespoons olive oil

2 garlic cloves, minced

2 scallions (green and white parts), chopped

1 large baking potato, peeled and diced

¼ teaspoon dried thyme

   Salt and freshly ground black pepper

2 cups corn kernels

6 eggs

1 cup coarsely shredded mozzarella or cheddar cheese (4 ounces)

2 tablespoons fresh flat-leaf parsley

Serves 4–6

I recently overheard Trainer tell a friend who came to dinner that a frittata is scrambled eggs baked in a pie. I cook frittatas when I have a lot of eggs, a lot of vegetables, and not much time. In the summer, we eat corn just about every day that it's available locally, and this is a good summer dish to use up leftover corn or potatoes, not to mention the eggs that the hens are happy to lay. It will also work well with frozen kernels in winter.

. . . .

HOW TO MAKE

1 Position an oven rack 3 inches from the broiler and preheat.

2 Heat the oil in a large cast-iron skillet over medium heat, and add the garlic, scallions, potato, thyme, and salt and pepper to taste. Cover and cook for 5 minutes, resisting the urge to stir. Remove the lid, flip the mixture so the other side can brown, and then cook for 5 minutes longer. Add the corn and cook for a few minutes longer, to heat through.

3 Beat the eggs in a medium bowl, then add the cheese, parsley, and salt and pepper. Pour into the skillet, stirring just to mix with the potatoes. Cook without stirring (shaking occasionally to loosen it) until the bottom is golden but the top is still runny, 8 to 10 minutes. Finish the frittata by placing it under the broiler and cooking about 2 minutes until the top is golden and set. Slide onto a serving plate.

Cock-a-Doodle-Don't

When Jock Reynolds, who is now director of the Yale University Art Gallery, was about nine, he tended six hens. One turned out to be a rooster and began waking up the neighborhood. Not wanting to lose his fledgling egg business, he chopped off the rooster's head, plucked and gutted it, and then sold the poor guy to his mother for 50 cents.

vegetarian Dishes

> *"A man's goose is cooked when he meets a chick who starts talking turkey."*
> — Taffy Tuttle, *Houston Post*, 1953

Losing a chicken is hard, no matter the sex or the age. The first one we lost when she was only two weeks old. It was our first batch of chicks, and we watched them every chance we got (they are so comical and cute). They were still fluffy little balls when it became apparent that one was sick. We watched her decline rapidly, trying what we knew to help her, and then one day we noticed the other chicks pecking her. It was survival of the fittest in that cardboard box. I was appalled. When it became clear that she wasn't going to make it and we needed to end her suffering, I was helpless. I couldn't kill a chicken. Joe took her down to the river that night. I couldn't imagine how he did it, but he told me that he whispered to her right before he sent her on her way. I loved him so much for that.

The worst time, however, was an incident none of us will forget. One gray, cold wintry day, the kind that makes you question why you live in the Berkshires, I picked up the kids from school, ran a few errands, and came home just before dusk. I had forgotten to take my cell phone, and as I drove up the driveway, before I'd even gotten out of the car or put it in the garage, my neighbor Tom Bump came hurrying over. Tom had been sitting at his living room window, watching and waiting for our car, and — God bless him — had even dug a path through the knee-deep snow that separated our houses so he could reach me before the kids got out of the car. He wanted to tell me that three Siberian huskies had broken free from their pen a few miles away, traveled across town, leapt over our fence, plowed through the netting, and attacked the chickens. It was a bloody sight, and he didn't want the kids to see it.

It turns out that dogs by themselves usually won't harm hens, but when there are three of them together, they act like a pack of

marauding wolves. The three dogs killed two chickens and maimed another. Only Tom's yelling and carrying on caused them to pause, but even he couldn't stop them, so he called the animal control officer, who in turn called the chief of police.

We live in a small town, and, not knowing where the kids or I were, the chief of police called the museum where my husband works. Joe was on an important conference call, so his secretary told the police chief she'd need to take a message.

"It's a chicken emergency," the chief of police bellowed. "Put him on."

Joe rushed out of the meeting, heart in his throat, thinking it somehow involved the kids. It turns out the kind-hearted officer just wanted to prevent the kids from seeing the massacre. We buried the chickens (well, if truth be told, in January in New England you take them into the woods and shovel snow on top), and I spent a fat hour on the phone trying to find a veterinarian who would treat the one bird that survived. We live in the country, and the local vet handles horses, dogs, cats, hamsters, llamas, geckos, bearded dragons, snakes, owls, ducks . . . but not chickens. I cajoled. I begged. I promised not to hold him liable if our chicken croaked. Finally, $189 later, on top of a two-hour wait, the vet saw her, and Joe came home with Hot Wheels alive . . . barely.

The next three nights found Joe and me hovering in the coop, one of us holding down the bird, the other giving her antibiotic shots in her chest cavity. She survived. Trainer thought it was worth $189. Joe was not so sure.

The experience filled Trainer with sorrow, and he vowed never to have animals again because he couldn't stand the pain of losing one. I understood completely. It took him awhile to come around to getting new chicks (Isabel was still avoiding them), but he agreed to try again the following spring, and since that "chicken emergency" we haven't lost many hens.

Trainer did get to the point where he resisted eating poultry, even if they weren't our chickens, and by the time he was in fourth grade he decided on his own to become a vegetarian. He convinced us to stop feeding the chickens any food scraps from our roast chicken — "We don't want to turn them into cannibals, Mom!"

With a vegetarian in the house, I found myself boning up more intently on nutrition basics. I saw it as an opportunity to inform myself and my children about wellness, the importance of protein, and the many ways they can get the nutrients they need, which is especially important as Trainer turns into a teenager and has to make food choices at school, parties, and friends' houses. Although estimates vary depending on the source, a nationwide survey by the Vegetarian Resource Group estimated that about 3 percent of American youth (1.4 million people between ages 8 and 18) are vegetarian.

This chapter contains vegetarian, kid-friendly, protein-rich recipes.

RED PEPPER & POTATO FRITTATA

INGREDIENTS

5 small potatoes

4 teaspoons extra-virgin olive oil

1 red bell pepper, seeded and diced or sliced

1 large onion, thinly sliced

2 garlic cloves, minced

8 eggs

2 tablespoons milk or half-and-half

1 teaspoon chopped fresh basil, oregano, flat-leaf parsley, or chives

¼ teaspoon salt

Freshly ground black pepper

¾ cup freshly grated Parmesan cheese (3 ounces)

Serves 4

This baked egg dish is a natural vehicle for incorporating whatever ingredients you have on hand, be they vegetables (asparagus, spinach, mushrooms, or Swiss chard may be substituted for the bell peppers), cheeses (fontina, cheddar, havarti, goat cheese), or meats (ham, bacon). Serve in wedges and refrigerate the leftovers for lunch the next day.

HOW TO MAKE

1 Bring a pot of salted water to a boil and cook the potatoes until tender and easily pierced with a knife, about 15 minutes. Drain, cool, and slice.

2 Preheat the oven to 350°F.

3 Heat 2 teaspoons of the olive oil in a 12-inch ovenproof skillet over medium heat. Sauté the bell pepper and onion until tender, about 10 minutes. Add the garlic and sauté for another minute. Transfer to a bowl and wipe the skillet.

4 Whisk the eggs, milk, basil, salt and pepper to taste in a separate bowl. Stir in the cheese.

5 Reheat the skillet with the remaining 2 teaspoons of olive oil over medium heat. Add the bell pepper and onion, stirring just to heat, then quickly layer the potatoes over the vegetables. Pour in the egg mixture, shaking gently to spread to all the cracks and crevices. Cook over medium heat, shaking occasionally, until the frittata has set on the bottom but is still liquid on top, about 10 minutes. Transfer to the oven and bake about 10 minutes, until the top is set. Remove from the oven and let sit for 5 minutes. Slide the frittata onto a platter and cut into wedges. Serve hot, at room temperature, or cold.

FRIDAY-NIGHT FRITTATA

Frittatas are perfect for the end of a busy week. Their merits are many: They only use one dish, they incorporate vegetables or whatever you have in your pantry, they take fewer than 20 minutes to prepare, and they make good leftovers.

· ·

INGREDIENTS

2 tablespoons extra-virgin olive oil

6 cups assorted chopped vegetables (such as bell peppers, broccoli, garlic, kale, mushrooms, onion, or spinach), kept separate

9 eggs

1–2 teaspoons chopped herbs, such as basil, cilantro, oregano, rosemary, or thyme

Salt and freshly ground black pepper

1½–2 cups crumbled or shredded cheese, such as cheddar, cottage cheese, feta, mozzarella, or ricotta

Serves 4

HOW TO MAKE

1 Preheat the broiler.

2 Heat an ovenproof skillet over medium heat, add the olive oil, then add the vegetables one at a time, stirring with a wooden spoon to prevent sticking, and sauté until cooked to your desired doneness. Because of their different cooking times, the choice of vegetables will determine the order you add them to the skillet; start the onions before kale, for example.

3 Lightly beat the eggs in a bowl with the herbs and the salt and pepper to taste, turn the heat under the skillet to high, then pour in the eggs. Cook for 1 minute. Lower the heat to medium and continue cooking until the eggs are almost set, about 5 minutes longer. Remove from the heat, sprinkle the cheese on top, and cook under the broiler 2 to 3 minutes, until the frittata is set. Serve immediately.

"I did not become a vegetarian for my health, I did it for the health of the chickens."

— Isaac Bashevis Singer

TURKISH POACHED EGGS WITH YOGURT

INGREDIENTS

1 cup 2% plain Greek yogurt

1 garlic clove, minced

Salt and freshly ground black pepper

4 tablespoons butter

10 fresh sage leaves

½ teaspoon paprika

½ teaspoon red pepper flakes

1 tablespoon white vinegar

8 eggs

Serves 4

Mama said there'd be days like this: You're running late, your kids are starving, you're low on food, you want to get dinner on the table in 20 minutes, soccer practice is in an hour, and you can't for the life of you think of what to cook. Poached eggs can save you. A staple of the Turkish diet, eggs offer a tremendous bang for the buck, as they're packed with protein and minerals, and they can be incorporated into dishes as easy as this one. Mix up the yogurt so you have it at the ready, whip up the eggs, then serve with some pita, naan, tortillas, or other bread to soak up the sauce.

HOW TO MAKE

1 Blend the yogurt and garlic in a small bowl, season to taste with salt and pepper, then set aside in the refrigerator for an hour or so. When ready to cook, divide the yogurt sauce among four plates, spreading it to make a large circle.

2 Melt the butter in a saucepan over medium heat, then add the sage, paprika, and red pepper flakes, stirring until the butter sizzles. Remove from the heat.

3 Bring 2 inches of water, or enough to submerge the eggs, to a simmer in a saucepan and add the vinegar. Crack the eggs into the water and simmer until they're softly cooked, about 3 minutes. Using a slotted spoon, remove the eggs from the water, drain briefly on paper towels, then put a pair of eggs atop each plate of yogurt. Rewarm the butter sauce if necessary, then spoon it over the eggs (leave the sage leaves in the pan) and serve.

EGG & BLACK BEAN TORTILLAS WITH CHIPOTLE CREAM SAUCE

INGREDIENTS

1 tablespoon vegetable oil

½ small white onion, diced

1 green or red bell pepper, seeded and diced

2 cups cooked black beans

1 tablespoon red hot sauce

1 teaspoon ground cumin

Salt

8 flour tortillas

6 eggs

½ cup Chipotle Cream Sauce (recipe follows)

2 avocados, pitted, peeled, and sliced

2 ripe tomatoes, chopped

1 cup shredded Mexican blend cheese

Serves 4

This recipe has three of my favorite ingredients: eggs, tortillas, and black beans. In our house, we eat tortillas as often as we eat bread. We're always using them to sop up the juice of a dish or to make a quick quesadilla. Isabel even likes a rolled tortilla in her lunch box as a snack. Black beans are high in protein, magnesium, manganese, potassium, calcium, folate, and iron.

. . . .

HOW TO MAKE

1 Preheat the oven to 350°F.

2 Heat the oil in a medium skillet and sauté the onion and bell pepper until soft, about 10 minutes. Add the beans, hot sauce, cumin, and salt to taste, and cook until the beans are heated.

3 While you are cooking the beans, wrap the tortillas in foil and warm in the oven for 10 minutes.

4 Beat the eggs in a bowl and scramble them in a medium nonstick skillet over medium heat, stirring frequently, until soft fluffy curds form, about 2 minutes.

5 Holding a tortilla in your hand, spoon a line of cream sauce down the center of the tortilla, then add some of the bean mixture and the eggs. Top with avocados, tomatoes, and cheese, then roll up. Repeat with the remaining tortillas; serve warm.

CHIPOTLE CREAM SAUCE

INGREDIENTS

1 cup sour cream

2–3 teaspoons Jump Up and Kiss Me Chipotle Sauce or other chipotle hot sauce

Makes 1 cup

While researching my first hot sauce cookbook in New Mexico, I discovered the marvelous chipotle, a dried chile made by smoking jalapeño peppers. These days, when we crank up the smoke pit in our backyard for a big rib fest, Joe will throw in a bunch of jalapeños to smoke, and in the winter I'll sometimes uncap the Ball jar we store them in just to get a rustic whiff. I fell so in love with chipotles that I started bottling my own sauce (Jump Up and Kiss Me Chipotle Sauce), which is an all-natural blend of roasted red bell peppers, raisins, and chipotles that you can find in gourmet stores or online from Dave's Gourmet. I've used my sauce here, although any chipotle sauce will do. Whether they're dried or in adobo sauce, chipotles add depth and a subtle smoky spiciness to a variety of dishes.

. . . .

HOW TO MAKE

Blend the sour cream and hot sauce in a small bowl.

SOUTHWESTERN EGG BURRITOS

INGREDIENTS

4 (8-inch) whole-wheat flour tortillas

4 eggs

1 tablespoon extra-virgin olive oil

1 small green, red, or yellow bell pepper, seeded and diced

1 small serrano chile, seeded and minced (or substitute chipotle chiles in adobo)

¾ cup shredded cheddar or Monterey jack cheese (3 ounces)

1 cup tomato salsa

Salt and freshly ground black pepper

Makes 4 burritos

The winter I wrote this book, we had eight major snowstorms — the snowiest winter on record, did the weatherman have to keep reminding us? — and it snowed right up to the hens' door. They wouldn't go outside, even though I shoveled a path for them and opened the door on warm days (we're talking 15°F) to give them fresh air. One morning I went out to the coop before breakfast, checked on the girls, cranked up their space heater, and gave them a consoling pat-pat-pat. They clucked without enthusiasm, giving me the brush-off with their bony shoulders. They were feeling cooped up, and I agreed. They barely gave me enough eggs for dinner.

That night I made simple burritos for the family, which I served with refried beans, avocados, and sour cream on the side, wishing we were someplace warm.

. . . .

HOW TO MAKE

1 Preheat the oven to 350°F. Wrap the tortillas in foil and heat for 10 minutes.

2 Blend the eggs in a medium bowl with a fork. Heat the oil in a nonstick or cast-iron skillet over medium heat, then sauté the bell pepper and chile until soft, about 5 minutes.

3 Lower the heat, add the eggs, and scramble, stirring frequently, until soft fluffy curds form, about 2 minutes. Lay the tortillas flat on plates and divide the eggs among them. Sprinkle each with the cheese, salsa, and salt and pepper to taste. Roll up and serve.

TURKISH PIZZA

INGREDIENTS

2 whole-wheat pitas, halved crosswise

2 tablespoons olive oil

Paprika

2 tablespoons butter or olive oil

1 bunch (10 ounces) fresh spinach

Kosher salt and freshly ground black pepper

4 eggs

½ cup crumbled feta cheese

1–2 tablespoons minced shallots

4 kalamata olives, pitted and chopped

Makes 4 pizzas (serves 2)

I have the best babysitter in the world (my kids would agree), but Cathy Dow doesn't like to cook and makes no bones about it. I gave her this recipe to try one night when I was running late and wouldn't be home in time to cook, and she obliged . . . and then asked for a copy of the recipe to take home. It's that easy and that good.

A popular street snack in Turkey, this pizza works well for lunch or supper. You can use pizza dough, though pitas are a fine substitute. For a heartier, non-vegetarian dish, sprinkle cooked lamb with spices on top of the spinach.

HOW TO MAKE

1 Preheat the oven to 425°F.

2 Place the pitas, cut-side up, on a baking sheet. Brush with the oil and sprinkle with some paprika.

3 Melt the butter in a skillet over medium heat. Add the spinach and the salt and pepper to taste, and cook until wilted, stirring frequently, about 2 minutes. Spread the spinach over the entire tops of the pitas, mounding it up a bit in the center so you can then make a well. Crack 1 egg into each well, then sprinkle with the cheese, shallots, and olives. Season with salt, pepper, and paprika.

4 Bake until the eggs are cooked to your liking, about 8 minutes for a runny yolk, taking care not to burn the pitas. Serve immediately.

INGREDIENTS

1 tablespoon butter

1 tablespoon minced shallot

1 pound fresh spinach, trimmed

  Salt and freshly ground black pepper

4 eggs

¼ cup freshly grated Parmesan cheese

2 English muffins or 4 slices of bread

Serves 4

EGGS FLORENTINE

In the 1500s, Caterina de' Medici, an heiress in Florence who eventually became queen of France, loved spinach so much that she supposedly called for it at every meal. To this day, any dish with the word *Florentine* in it means there's spinach included. Part of the Benedict family, Eggs Florentine can be served for breakfast, though they also make a delicious supper.

• •

HOW TO MAKE

1 Preheat the oven to 350°F.

2 Heat the butter in a large skillet over medium heat and sauté the shallot until softened, a few minutes. Add the spinach and cover, stirring occasionally, and cook until wilted, 2 to 3 minutes. Remove from the heat, let cool, and then drain. Squeeze out any moisture, then chop.

3 Butter a small baking dish and spread the spinach in it, making four indentations. Season with salt and pepper to taste. Gently crack 1 egg into each nest, and then sprinkle on the Parmesan.

4 Bake for 15 minutes, or until the egg whites are just set.

5 Toast the English muffins and top each half with some spinach and an egg. Serve immediately.

GREEK OMELET

Julia Child once defined an omelet as soft-scrambled eggs wrapped in an envelope of firmly cooked scrambled eggs.

Originally from the Near East, versions of omelets appear in many cultures, from the Italian frittata to the Spanish tortilla to the French omelet. I didn't often think of serving omelets until we started raising chickens and got a lot of eggs. If there are vegetarians in your household, an omelet is a handy way to incorporate vegetables and protein into a main dish. Add a salad and some fruit, and you've got a wholesome meal.

This recipe lends itself to experimenting: substitute kale for the spinach, or add potatoes and red bell peppers.

INGREDIENTS

1 tablespoon olive oil

1 small yellow onion, chopped

4 eggs

1 teaspoon fresh oregano leaves

½ cup crumbled feta cheese

¼ cup chopped cooked spinach

Salt and freshly ground black pepper

Serves 2

HOW TO MAKE

1 Heat the olive oil in a nonstick skillet over medium heat and cook the onion, stirring frequently until caramelized, about 20 minutes.

2 Beat the eggs in a bowl with the oregano, then pour into the skillet over the onion. Crumble the cheese over the eggs and sprinkle with the spinach. When the eggs are mostly set, fold the omelet in half (with either a spatula or a deft flip of the skillet). Slide the omelet onto a warm plate, season with salt and pepper to taste, and serve at once.

Omelet Tips

+ If you're serving more than one person, make individual omelets rather than one big one. Wipe out the pan with paper towels after each omelet; never clean it with soap and water in between cooking the omelets.

+ If you like salt in your omelet, add it after the omelet is cooked; salting the eggs before cooking can cause them to toughen. If you are adding other flavorings, such as herbs and truffle shavings, do so to the beaten eggs before you cook them.

+ According to Julia Child, never use any liquid fillings or liquid-producing fillings such as tomatoes, as they will make your omelet, in her words, "just a mess."

CLASSIC FRENCH OMELET

INGREDIENTS

2–3 eggs

1 tablespoon milk

1–2 teaspoons butter

¼ cup shredded cheese of your choice

Salt and freshly ground black pepper

Serves 1

You can serve this plain or add 2 to 3 tablespoons of filling such as sautéed wild mushrooms, Canadian bacon, spinach, blue cheese, salmon, parsley, or diced apples. Your filling can be fresh or cooked, sweet or savory. I've even added onion jam, with good results.

• •

HOW TO MAKE

1 Beat the eggs and milk in a bowl with a fork or a whisk until blended.

2 Melt a pat of butter in a cast-iron or nonstick skillet over medium to high heat. When the butter stops foaming, pour in the eggs, swirling the pan to distribute them. Cook, lifting the sides of the omelet to let the uncooked egg flow underneath, until almost set, about 2 minutes (the top should still be slightly uncooked, like a custard). Quickly sprinkle the cheese over half of the omelet, fold the plain side over the cheese, and cook for 20 seconds longer. Slide the omelet onto a warm plate, season with salt and pepper to taste, and serve.

"No clever arrangement of bad eggs ever made a good omelet."

— C. S. Lewis

MACARONI & CHEESE

INGREDIENTS

1 pound elbow macaroni

3 slices bread

½ teaspoon dried thyme

2 tablespoons butter

4 cups milk

6 egg yolks

4 cups shredded cheddar cheese (1 pound)

1 tablepoon dry mustard

1 teaspoon salt

¼ teaspoon freshly ground black pepper

Serves 8

Every woman should be blessed with a girlfriend like Janette Dudley. We met 13 years ago when our sons, practically infants, were in a playgroup (the boys are still close friends), and then we were doubly fortunate when, several years later, our daughters became good friends, as did our husbands. We've enjoyed a friendship over the years that's included travel, playground time, skiing, parenting, town issues, Super Bowl parties, and a quest for the perfect mac and cheese. Janette turned me on to an excellent recipe, which I've tweaked here to include eggs for my vegetarian son.

. . . .

HOW TO MAKE

1 Bring a large pot of salted water to a boil and cook the macaroni according to the package directions. Drain and let cool slightly.

2 Preheat the oven to 350ºF. Grease a 9- by 13-inch baking dish.

3 Toast the bread, break it into pieces, and chop it coarsely in a food processor with the thyme (and a little salt and pepper, if desired). Melt the butter in a small saucepan, add the breadcrumbs, and toss to coat evenly.

4 Combine the milk and egg yolks in a large bowl, then add the cheese, dry mustard, salt, and pepper. Add the macaroni and stir to combine. Spoon the macaroni mixture into the prepared baking dish.

5 Top the macaroni with the breadcrumbs and bake for 1 hour, or until the top is golden and crusty. Let stand for 10 minutes before serving.

VEGETARIAN DISHES

ENCHILADAS

INGREDIENTS

2 tablespoons vegetable oil

1 garlic clove

2 (10-ounce) cans diced tomatoes with green chiles

6 small (6- to 8-inch) flour tortillas

4 eggs

Salt and freshly ground black pepper

1 bunch scallions, chopped

½ cup shredded cheddar cheese

Serves 3

Several years ago, we took a fantastic family trip to Mexico. Exploring the Mayan ruins, we drove from Chichén Itzá to Coba, where we rode bikes from one edifice to the next, and then on to the coastal ruins of Tulum. Eating local dishes at cafés in small towns along the way, we sampled delicious, simple Mexican cooking. I've tried to replicate here one of the tasty dishes we enjoyed.

. . . .

HOW TO MAKE

1 To make the sauce, heat 1 tablespoon of the oil in a small skillet and sauté the garlic for a minute or two. Add the tomatoes and simmer for 10 minutes. Set aside.

2 Preheat the oven to 350°F.

3 Heat the remaining 1 tablespoon of oil in a skillet and fry each tortilla briefly on both sides (essentially to cook them slightly and warm them).

4 Beat the eggs in a small bowl, season with the salt and pepper, and then scramble over medium heat in a skillet, stirring frequently until soft fluffy curds form, about 2 minutes.

5 Lay the tortillas on a flat surface, divide the scrambled eggs among them, sprinkle each with 2 teaspoons of scallions, and roll up. Put them in a 9- by 13-inch baking dish, pour the sauce over each, sprinkle the cheese on top, then follow with the remaining scallions. Bake for 20 minutes, or until heated through.

ROASTED ASPARAGUS WITH POACHED EGGS & MISO BUTTER

INGREDIENTS

2 handfuls thin asparagus, trimmed

Extra-virgin olive oil

Salt

1 tablespoon unsalted butter, softened

1 tablespoon light miso paste

½ teaspoon sherry vinegar

2 poached eggs (see page 41)

Salt and freshly cracked black peppercorns

Serves 2

When this dish was served at Momofuku, *New York Magazine* rated it one of the 10 best egg dishes in the city. This is adapted from David Chang's marvelous recipe.

HOW TO MAKE

1 Preheat the oven to 450°F.

2 Coat the asparagus with the olive oil, sprinkle with salt, and spread in a single layer on an edged baking sheet. Roast about 10 minutes, until tender.

3 Blend the butter, miso paste, and sherry vinegar in a small bowl.

4 To serve, divide the miso butter between two plates and top each with half of the roasted asparagus and 1 egg. Season with salt and the cracked pepper.

ZUCCHINI FRITTERS

INGREDIENTS

2 medium zucchini, trimmed and coarsely shredded

2 eggs

1 large garlic clove, minced

4 scallions, chopped

¼ cup unbleached all-purpose flour

2 tablespoons freshly grated Parmesan cheese

½ teaspoon salt

¼ teaspoon freshly ground black pepper

5 tablespoons extra-virgin olive oil

Sour cream

Makes 12 fritters

Because our house is tucked into a hillside, the flower garden is just below the ledge of the kitchen window. One day we were sitting at the kitchen table, eating fritters for lunch, with the chickens roaming free, when we looked out and there was a hen perched on the window ledge, staring in at us curiously. I was glad she hasn't discovered just how tasty her eggs are.

. . . .

HOW TO MAKE

1 Remove the excess moisture from the zucchini by squeezing them in a clean cotton kitchen towel.

2 Whisk the eggs in a large bowl and add the zucchini, garlic, scallions, flour, Parmesan, salt, and pepper. Stir well to combine.

3 Heat the oil in a large skillet. Drop half the batter by rounded tablespoonfuls into the skillet, flattening each fritter slightly. Cook, turning once, until browned, 4 to 6 minutes on each side. Transfer to paper towels to drain. Repeat with the remaining batter. Serve hot with sour cream on the side.

BAKED EGGS IN TOMATOES

INGREDIENTS

4 large tomatoes

Salt and freshly ground black pepper

4 eggs

¼ cup toasted breadcrumbs, preferably homemade

¼ cup freshly grated Parmesan cheese

2 tablespoons chopped fresh flat-leaf parsley

Serves 4

Every year by late summer, I'm yearning for the tomato harvest at Caretaker, our community farm. In good years, the tomato crop is bountiful, and we're canning enough sauce to last the winter; in lean years, with bad weather and blight, we pick barely enough for a fresh tomato pasta dinner. When the tomatoes are perfect and plentiful, this dish is delicious for brunch or with fish at dinner.

HOW TO MAKE

1 Preheat the oven to 400°F.

2 Cut off the tops of the tomatoes, scoop out the seeds and membranes, and place in a shallow baking dish. Season the cavities with salt and pepper. Gently crack an egg into each tomato.

3 Bake 25 to 30 minutes, until the eggs are set. With 2 or 3 minutes to go, sprinkle the breadcrumbs and Parmesan on top of the eggs. Remove from the oven and sprinkle with the parsley before serving.

To Everything There Is a Season

One Monday in March, we had our first taste of spring . . . the temperature rose to 60 degrees, causing a rushing river in front of the house as the mountain snows melted into the Hoosac River. I let the chickens out of their pen — they'd been snowbound for weeks — and they were ecstatic. I even let them go in my flower beds; I couldn't bring myself to scold them.

That night Trainer tucked them into the coop, and when I went to let them out the next morning, I found one hovering at the outside of the door. I asked Trainer; he'd shut up the coop after dark, so she should have gotten back in. She got either confused or lost. Something was not quite right.

The next day I found her huddled in the corner of the coop, under a ledge, while the others were outside foraging. She was our oldest hen — five years old, which by chicken standards is ancient — and had seen flocks of chicks come and go. She was a survivor. On Wednesday the other girls went out again, and I found her huddled in the corner, this time accompanied by the gentle Buff Orpington, who hovered next to her, clearly a sign of camaraderie, trying to offer the comfort of being nearby even when there was nothing she could do.

On Thursday, Trainer checked them and came back reporting that all the girls were inside huddled around her. Clearly she was not right; her eyes were half shut and had a glazed quality. I held her, then gave up as it didn't seem particularly comforting to her (would she prefer me or her hens? I wondered). Trainer went out and cuddled her in a sweatshirt for a while, too. I left the heat on and lifted her onto her perch, sandwiched between two big fat hens.

The next morning I went out and she was dead in a hammock made by chicken wire under the perch. Four chickens were hovering over her on the perch, making low, rather mournful squawks, vulture-like priests issuing last rites. I wish I had a camera as Joe went up there, in suit, starched white shirt, and cuff links — all ready to go out and have an important meeting or ask someone for money — and disposed of the old gal. That afternoon the Buff Orpington seemed really sad. I picked her up and patted her and she rested her head on my arm, as if to say, "I *am* sad."

POPOVERS

INGREDIENTS

3 tablespoons butter, chilled

4 eggs

1¼ cups milk

2 tablespoons butter, melted

1¼ cups unbleached all-purpose flour

¼ teaspoon salt

Makes 10 popovers

Popovers remind me of the Jordan Pond House on Mount Desert Island in Maine, where they are exquisite served with jam or ice cream at afternoon tea. They also take me back to my childhood, when we'd go to Anthony's Pier 4 in Boston for super-special occasions, and I thought it was the ultimate in sophistication that suited men came around to our table, serving them from enormous baskets with tongs. They're so easy to make and are a great snack or teatime treat. Or add a bit of Parmesan cheese to the batter and serve with a roast.

HOW TO MAKE

1 Preheat the oven to 375°F. Butter a six-cup popover pan. Add ½ tablespoon of the chilled butter to the bottom of each cup and put the pan in the oven until the butter melts.

2 Beat the eggs until foamy using an electric mixer. Beat in the milk and melted butter and reduce the speed to low. Add the flour and salt and beat until smooth, about 3 minutes.

3 Fill the prepared popover pan cups three-quarters of the way with batter and bake 35 to 40 minutes, until puffed and well browned. Serve immediately.

DID YOU REMEMBER THE CHICKENS?

Desserts

"Tomorrow is a busy day
We got things to do, we got eggs to lay
Ground to dig, and worms to scratch
It takes a lot of sittin', gettin' chicks to hatch
Besides — there ain't nobody here but us chickens
There ain't nobody here at all
So quiet yourself and stop that fuss
Hey there ain't nobody here but us"

— Alex Kramer and Joan Whitney,
  "Ain't Nobody Here But Us Chickens"

There seems to be an inescapable progression from chickens to bees to tree-tapping to knitting to . . . I'm glad we aren't tempted by llamas. But we do live with ten chickens, 80,000 bees, a cat named Wylie Jefferson, and a leopard gecko named Spot. They are all our pets (well, maybe not the bees). If anyone had ever told me that I'd talk to chickens, greet them in the morning, coo to them, call them "my girls," tuck them into my chest, and stroke their ruffled feathers when they need calming, I'd have called that person crazy. But I caught the bug.

I'm not alone. The renowned children's illustrator Jan Brett has 60 chickens, and when she drives from Boston to her summer cottage in the Berkshires, she fits them all into her husband's Jaguar and her Prius uncaged — these are free-roaming gals on the Mass Pike. "We get a lot of looks when we stop for gas," she says. Their henhouse — think nineteenth-century Norwegian chalet, decorated with real flowers and painted illustrations — has piped-in classical music, which is not surprising given that her husband is a bassist with the Boston Symphony Orchestra, and she visits with them regularly to kiss them and massage their feet. (Meanwhile, one morning before I drove my teenage son to school and said good-bye to the hens, Trainer looked at me and said, "Mom, it's sorta weird to talk to your chickens.") When Jan works late into the night to create her lavish illustrations, at least one hen is perched on her shoulder while she labors at the drawing table.

We live in the cult of the hen, the year of the chicken. When we
started raising chickens, most nights at dinner Joe and I would look
at each other and one of us would inevitably say, "Did you remember
the chickens?" In other words, did someone remember to close up
the coop and put on their night-light? Familiar with wall signage
from having worked in museums over the years, we had the saying
stenciled in large, putty-colored letters on a beam in our kitchen, so
that you see it when you first walk into the house.

Given that Joe is director of MASS MoCA, we often invite home to
dinner artists who are making work there. Isabel has bounced on
the knee of Bill T. Jones and made drawings with Leonard Nimoy.
Trainer has built with Legos with Matthew Ritchie and introduced
our chickens to Gregory Crewdson's kids. One December, the celebrated Chinese artist Cai Guo-Qiang was in the Berkshires, making
a huge ambitious artwork that featured nine cars hurtling through
space in a cinematic progression down MASS MoCA's largest gallery.
It was his birthday and he was alone in the snowy Berkshires, away
from his family. From Beijing, Cai Guo-Qiang was born in the year of
the rooster, and when he came into our house that freezing night on
his birthday far away from home, the first thing he saw was "Did you
remember the chickens?" When his translator interpreted the sign,
he shuddered visibly, reflected for a moment, and then his shoulders
relaxed perceptibly. I think he decided we were A-OK. After all, we
raised chickens.

NUT WAFERS

This recipe is from my grandmother, who was born in 1899 and as a young woman attended Fannie Farmer's cooking school in Boston. Wafer thin, this is a nutty teatime sweet.

. . . .

INGREDIENTS

1 cup pecans or walnuts, finely chopped

1 cup lightly packed brown sugar

3 tablespoons unbleached all-purpose flour

Pinch of salt

2 eggs

Makes 24 wafers

HOW TO MAKE

1 Preheat the oven to 350°F. Spray a baking sheet with nonstick cooking spray.

2 Combine the nuts, sugar, flour, salt, and eggs in a medium bowl and mix. Drop the dough by teaspoonsful onto the prepared baking sheet, about 3 inches apart, and bake for 10 minutes, until golden around the edges. Let cool on a wire rack.

GRAPE-NUT PUDDING

INGREDIENTS

2 eggs

2 cups whole milk

1 teaspoon vanilla extract

Pinch of salt

½ cup sugar

½ cup Grape-Nuts cereal

Serves 4

Every family party, holiday, or birthday, my grandmother would make grape-nut pudding for dessert, and we'd eat the leftovers for breakfast. I still have her recipe card with her faded (but perfectly clear) instructions, which I've transcribed below. If you want to go all out, grate some fresh nutmeg into the batter. I use a 7-inch round pan for this old-fashioned New England staple, which is delicious served warm or cold, with a splash of milk or half-and-half.

• •

HOW TO MAKE

1 Preheat the oven to 350°F. Grease a 7- or 8-inch round or square baking dish.

2 Beat the eggs in a medium bowl. Add the milk, vanilla, and salt and blend. Add the sugar and Grape-Nuts and mix well. Transfer the mixture to the prepared baking dish and bake for 45 minutes, or until a knife inserted in the middle comes out clean. Let cool slightly before serving.

"She was not like other chickens. She didn't fight my grasp or spurn my affection. She sat in my lap like a well-fed cat, tucked up her claws, puffed out her feathers, lowered her eyelids and — I swear — started to purr. Not exactly like a cat's purr, muffled but audible, but a silent purr, more chicken-like."

— Michelle Madden, The Sweet Beet blog

DESSERTS

VANILLA PUDDING

INGREDIENTS

½ cup sugar

3 tablespoons cornstarch

⅛ teaspoon salt

4 eggs

2½ cups half-and-half or whole milk

1½ teaspoons vanilla extract

Freshly grated nutmeg or chocolate shavings

Serves 4–6

In the summertime, when the weather's fine, the hens hunt all day long for grub in the yard. You can hear them clucking contentedly, looking up at me expectantly as I come near to pet them or snip some chives in the garden. A young hen on a warm day is a prodigious layer, and this velvety-smooth dessert is easy to whip up when you've got plenty of eggs. As Cervantes said, the proof of the pudding is in the eating.

HOW TO MAKE

1 Combine the sugar, cornstarch, and salt in a medium saucepan. Whip the eggs and half-and-half in a medium bowl to combine, then stir into the saucepan. Turn the heat to medium and cook, stirring constantly, until the mixture thickens, about 10 minutes. Do not boil.

2 Remove from the heat, stir in the vanilla, and pour into four to six individual dishes. Chill for a few hours before serving; cover the surface with plastic wrap before refrigerating if you don't like skin on top of your pudding. Serve with freshly grated nutmeg or shaved chocolate on top.

RICE PUDDING

Found in most cultures, boiled or baked, rice pudding is a simple dish consisting of rice, milk, sweetener, and flavoring. Our son, Trainer, loves the rice pudding at a local restaurant. When the restaurant refused to divulge how it was made, I went on a hunt for the best rice pudding recipe. My family settled on this one, which is adapted from one used by the historic Red Lion Inn in Stockbridge, Massachusetts.

INGREDIENTS

2½ cups whole milk

⅓ cup uncooked white rice

⅛ teaspoon salt

⅓ cup brown sugar

1 egg

1 teaspoon vanilla extract

¼ teaspoon ground cinnamon

Serves 2–3

HOW TO MAKE

1 Combine the milk, rice, and salt in a medium saucepan and bring to a boil. Reduce the heat to low and simmer until the rice is tender, stirring frequently, about 20 minutes.

2 Whisk the sugar and egg in a small bowl, then add ½ cup of the cooked rice, 1 tablespoon at a time, stirring vigorously. Add the egg mixture to the saucepan and stir over low heat until thick, about 10 minutes. Do not boil. Stir in the vanilla. Remove from the heat and stir in the cinnamon. Let cool slightly before serving.

PANETTONE BREAD PUDDING

INGREDIENTS

Butter

2 cups heavy cream

2 cups whole milk

1 vanilla bean

Zest of 1 orange

4 eggs

¾ cup sugar

¼ teaspoon freshly grated nutmeg

1 loaf panettone, sliced thick

Confectioners' sugar

Serves 6

Variations: Just before you bake the panettone, sprinkle ½ cup of dried chopped dates or currants on top of the bread . . . or a few chopped plums . . . or prunes soaked in grappa.

If you can't find vanilla beans, substitute 1 teaspoon of vanilla extract.

If you can't find panettone, substitute challah.

One Christmas season, a guest brought us two large panettones, the traditional fruit bread served in Italy at the holidays and other festive occasions such as weddings and christenings. I greatly enjoyed the first loaf, then wondered aloud what to do with the second, which was going stale on my counter, when my friend Eric Kerns tipped me off to this glorious dessert. Among its amazing features: It is easy to make, it appears elegant, and it has the comforting quality of gussied-up French toast.

HOW TO MAKE

1 Preheat the oven to 325°F. Butter a 9- by 13-inch baking dish.

2 Pour the cream and milk into a saucepan over medium heat and bring to a simmer. Slice the vanilla bean in half, scrape out the seeds, and add the seeds and pod to the pan, along with the orange zest.

3 Whisk the eggs with the sugar in a medium bowl until thick and pale, 3 to 4 minutes. Add the milk mixture, after removing the vanilla pod. Sprinkle in the nutmeg.

4 Butter one side of each slice of the panettone. Dunk into the milk mixture and layer in the prepared baking dish (buttered-side up). Ladle the remaining milk mixture over the bread. Place the baking dish in a large roasting pan and carefully pour hot water into the roasting pan until halfway up the sides of the baking dish.

5 Bake for 45 minutes, or until the crust is golden (the inside will still be jiggly). Let cool slightly, then dust with confectioners' sugar to serve.

CREAMY EGG CUSTARD

INGREDIENTS

2 cups whole milk

2 eggs, at room-temperature

⅓ cup sifted confectioners' sugar

1 teaspoon vanilla extract

Freshly grated nutmeg

Serves 6

The secret to a silky custard is using sifted confectioners' sugar and eggs that are at room temperature. If you want to speed up the warming process, run the eggs under warm water from the tap, which will loosen the protein inside.

. . . .

HOW TO MAKE

1 Preheat the oven to 350°F. Set six 3-inch ramekins in a roasting pan large enough to hold them and a water bath.

2 Bring the milk to a near boil (don't let it boil) in a heavy pan. While you are heating the milk, whisk the eggs, sugar, and vanilla in a bowl using a handheld electric mixer on low speed. Add the milk slowly, blending after each addition.

3 Pour the mixture through a fine-mesh strainer into the ramekins (if it clogs, scrape clean with a spoon) and top with grated nutmeg. Carefully pour hot water into the baking dish around the ramekins until it is even with the level of custard in the ramekins. Bake for about 1 hour, until the custard is set. Remove from the oven and cool on a rack for 1 hour.

The Good, the Bad, and the Rooster

One spring afternoon, the local day-care center called; they had hatched chicks as a science project and were looking to find a home for them. When you buy day-old chicks from a hatchery, they can tell you the sex with 99 percent certainty. This time the chicks weren't sexed, but I was a sucker and said I'd take four chicks . . . and we ended up with two roosters.

It wasn't obvious at first, but I distinctly remember the day I became suspicious. I was still asleep (it was barely light out) when I awoke to an *ert* in the backyard. "What was that?" I asked my husband. "Something in the woods," he mumbled, turning over. The next day it was a bit more pronounced: *ert ert*. Trainer noticed that two of the chicks were growing faster than the others ("must be the breed") and sported longer, more beautiful tail feathers (*that* should have been a dead giveaway). The *ert ert* grew in volume and the enunciation improved over the next few days, until one morning it was an obvious crowing from the kings of the roost.

There are advantages to having roosters: They are territorial and will protect your girls. Roosters are big and gorgeous, not to mention cocky, which is comforting when a winter fox trots across your yard in broad daylight and eyes the coop, then casts a sly sidelong glance in your direction, just like in the storybooks. We had lost several chickens to raccoons and it was a grisly experience, but since the roosters entered the coop we hadn't lost one. But, spaghetti westerns aside, there's the good, the bad, and the ugly. And when they are bad, they are very, very bad. They will attack your kids.

One warm day, the chickens were roaming around the yard while Trainer and Isabel played outside and I was sweeping the coop. All of a sudden, Chicken King (aptly named, it turned out) ran toward Isabel, rearing back on his hind legs so he stood as tall as my daughter, and attacked her, clawing at her face and stomach. I looked like the Wicked Witch of the West as I whacked him with my broom and chased him around the yard. Isabel was fine, although shaken and a little scratched, and it was a few years before she'd go near the chickens again.

We clearly had to get rid of him, though Trainer made the sad-eyed case that the animal was only acting instinctively and shouldn't end up in someone's pot. It was then that I discovered a chicken-owner's woe: it's hard to off-load a rooster. My friend Lauren Gotlieb, who is braver than I, offered to give me a lesson in "processing" a bird, which she'd just done with Andy the Rooster, afterward giving it to her mom to cook. The bird was a bit tough, and when Grandma fed a piece of it to Lauren's three-year-old son, he coughed. She asked if he was okay and he responded, "Yeah, I'm just choking on Andy."

In the end, we gave Chicken King to our local CSA farm, extracting a promise from Elisabeth, one of the owners, that Chicken King would live out a natural life on the farm with his fellow Rhode Island Reds. Elisabeth and her husband, Sam, are sensitive, wise people who love and understand kids. Trainer was satisfied, and we spent a comical afternoon (while Isabel hovered in the house, watching us through the kitchen window) chasing Chicken King around the yard, trying to catch and force him into a big cardboard box, which we then used to ferry him to the farm.

Unfortunately, with many animals to care for, Elisabeth forgot her promise over the winter. When we arrived in the spring to pick rhubarb, Trainer headed for the coop to visit Chicken King. When he asked where the rooster was, Elisabeth said easily, "Oh, he ended up in the pot," as if that was the most natural answer on a farm. Which it is.

It's best not to get chicks from a day-care science project, no matter how cute they are.

CHERRY CLAFOUTI

1 teaspoon unsalted butter

1 tablespoon plus ½ cup granulated sugar

1¼ cups whole milk

⅔ cup sifted unbleached all-purpose flour

3 eggs

2 teaspoons vanilla extract

⅛ teaspoon salt

2 cups pitted fresh cherries

Confectioners' sugar

Serves 8–10

This classic French dessert can best be described as a fruit-filled, lightly sweetened flan. Pronounced kla-foo-TEE, it is traditionally made with whole fresh cherries, but that can be dangerous for unsuspecting diners, so this version uses pitted fruit. You can also prepare this dessert with apples, pears, or berries. Out of season, use thawed frozen or canned cherries that are patted dry, but remember, the better tasting the fruit, the better the dish.

HOW TO MAKE

1   Preheat the oven to 375°F. Butter a 9-inch deep tart or pie plate. Sprinkle with the 1 tablespoon of granulated sugar and shake the pan to coat.

2   Combine the milk, flour, eggs, vanilla, the ½ cup of granulated sugar, and the salt in a blender. Blend until well combined, scraping down the sides if necessary. Pour a ¼-inch layer of batter into the prepared baking dish. Bake for 5 to 7 minutes, or until a film of batter has set in the bottom of the dish. Remove from the oven and arrange the cherries evenly in the batter in the bottom. Top with the remaining batter.

3   Bake for 25 to 35 minutes, or until puffed and golden and a knife inserted in the center comes out clean. Transfer to a wire rack and let cool slightly (it might shrink as it cools). Dust with confectioners' sugar just before serving.

CHOCOLATE SOUFFLÉ

INGREDIENTS

Butter

⅓ cup granulated sugar, plus more for dusting the pan

3 egg yolks

2 ounces bittersweet baking chocolate, coarsely chopped and melted

½ teaspoon vanilla extract

4 egg whites

Pinch of cream of tartar

Pinch of salt

Confectioners' sugar

Serves 4–6

For years I avoided making a soufflé, which loosely translated means "full of air." It was just too intimidating. What if it collapsed? How deflating. But then one Christmas my children saw a gorgeous chocolate soufflé on the cover of a food magazine in the checkout line and suggested we make it together for the holiday. How could I resist? Adding an extra egg white or two helps with the puffiness.

HOW TO MAKE

1 Preheat the oven to 350°F. Butter a 4-cup soufflé or deep baking dish and tap and rotate some granulated sugar into it to coat the bottom and sides.

2 Beat the egg yolks with three-quarters of the granulated sugar using an electric mixer until very light and thick. Stir in the melted chocolate and the vanilla. Using clean beaters, beat the egg whites with the cream of tartar and the salt in a separate bowl until soft peaks form. Add the remaining granulated sugar and continue to beat until stiff and glossy. Stir a spatula full of the whites into the chocolate base, then gently fold in the rest of the whites.

3 Transfer the mixture to the prepared baking dish (you may cover and refrigerate it for several hours at this point). Bake 25 to 30 minutes, until puffed and firm but still wobbly in the center. Dust with confectioners' sugar, then serve immediately.

CARUSO'S CHOCOLATE SOUFFLÉ

INGREDIENTS

Butter

4 eggs, separated

2 tablespoons confectioners' sugar, plus more for garnish (optional)

2 heaping tablespoons unsweetened cocoa powder

4–6 tablespoons cherry preserves

Serves 2

A few years ago I found this recipe of my mother's, with a note that she had tasted it at the Hotel Caruso Belvedere in Ravello, Italy, on the Amalfi Coast, and asked the chef for the recipe. By the way, a lot of recipes say "Serve immediately"; with soufflés, it really matters.

• •

HOW TO MAKE

1 Preheat the oven to 350°F. Butter two 4-ounce individual baking dishes.

2 Beat the egg whites with an electric mixer until stiff peaks form. Add the yolks and stir gently to combine. Gradually add the sugar and then the cocoa powder, mixing carefully.

3 Spread a thin layer of preserves on the bottom of each baking dish. Carefully spoon the chocolate mixture over the preserves. Bake about 12 minutes, until the soufflé rises but the center is still saucelike. Sprinkle with the sugar, if using, and serve immediately.

LEMON SOUFFLÉ

INGREDIENTS

Butter

4 egg yolks

1 cup sugar

Juice and zest of 1 lemon

4 egg whites

Serves 6

Several years ago I unearthed an old wooden box that had been my mother's. Inside were recipes with her handwriting, my grandmother's handwriting, and my great-grandmother's handwriting. This one dates back to the turn of the last century, when Anna Sherlock Harvey lived in Wellesley Hills, Massachusetts, and, in addition to raising seven children, was very socially engaged. This simple dessert will melt in your mouth.

. . . .

HOW TO MAKE

1 Preheat the oven to 350°F. Butter a 7-inch round baking dish.

2 Using an electric mixer, beat the egg yolks until thick and lemon colored. Gradually add the sugar and continue beating. Add the lemon juice and zest.

3 Beat the egg whites in a clean dry bowl, using an electric mixer, until stiff and glossy, then fold them gently into the yolk mixture. Turn into the prepared baking dish. Set in a roasting pan, carefully pour hot water into the roasting pan to create a water bath, and bake for 35 minutes, or until puffed and golden. Serve immediately.

VERNA'S SOUFFLÉ GLACÉ AU CITRON

This frothy dessert is "like lemon whipped cream," my son exclaimed, and especially welcome in warm weather, given that it is both light and tart, both creamy and smooth. With a few fresh berries and a sprig of mint, served in crystal stemmed glasses, it makes an elegant dinner-party dessert.

INGREDIENTS

6 egg yolks

1¼ cups sugar

¾ cup fresh lemon juice (4–5 lemons)

Grated zest of 2 lemons, plus more for garnish (optional)

1 tablespoon powdered gelatin, softened in ⅓ cup cold water

4 egg whites, at room temperature

1 cup heavy cream

Fresh berries (optional)

Fresh mint (optional)

Serves 8–10

HOW TO MAKE

1 Beat the egg yolks lightly in a heavy medium saucepan, then gradually beat in ¾ cup of the sugar. Stir in the lemon juice and grated zest. Cook over low heat, stirring continuously until the mixture has thickened to a light custard and coats a wooden spoon, 15 to 20 minutes. Do not let it boil. Remove from the heat immediately and stir in the gelatin and water. Pour into a bowl set in ice water to cool and prevent further cooking. Stir frequently until cooled. Chill in the refrigerator until the mixture becomes syrupy but not set, 10 to 15 minutes (watch carefully or you will regret it).

2 Beat the egg whites using an electric mixer until they form soft peaks. Gradually beat in the remaining ½ cup of the sugar to make a soft meringue. Whip the cream in a separate bowl, using an electric mixer, until it forms soft peaks (do not overbeat or it will not blend with the other ingredients). Add the whipped cream to the beaten egg whites in a large bowl. Pour the syrupy lemon custard over the cream. Using a slotted spoon, carefully fold the whole mixture together until smoothly blended.

3 Lightly oil a 1-quart soufflé dish and affix a paper collar to the inner rim so that it extends 4 inches above the rim. Pour the soufflé mixture into the dish. Chill for 4 to 8 hours, or put in the freezer for 1 hour 30 minutes, then refrigerate until serving. To serve, carefully remove the paper collar. Garnish with berries or a dusting of lemon zest.

TIPSY SQUIRE

INGREDIENTS

1 loaf sponge cake or pound cake

⅛–¼ cup sherry, rum, or brandy

2 cups whole milk, plus more as needed

¼ cup sugar

2 eggs, separated

1 tablespoon cornstarch

1 teaspoon vanilla extract

Whipped cream

Freshly grated nutmeg or blanched sliced almonds

Serves 6–8

I'd make this dessert for the name alone. A nineteenth-century southern version of the English trifle, the Tipsy Squire, which in some quarters is also known as the Tipsy Parson, is a way to use up leftover sponge cake. Stale cake works even better because it absorbs the liquid and doesn't get mushy. Make it the day before a party and refrigerate overnight.

. . . .

HOW TO MAKE

1 Invert the cake into a glass serving bowl and drizzle with the sherry.

2 Heat the milk in the top of a double boiler until it is almost boiling. Beat the sugar and egg yolks in a bowl. In a separate bowl, beat the egg whites into a stiff froth and then fold into the egg-yolk mixture.

3 Moisten the cornstarch with a little cold milk as needed until smooth and then gradually stir into the hot milk. Stir constantly until it thickens. Add the sugar and egg mixture and stir for a moment, then remove from the heat and let cool. Add the vanilla. Pour over the cake, cover, and refrigerate overnight.

4 When ready to serve, top each serving with a dollop of whipped cream and freshly grated nutmeg or almonds.

CARROT CAKE

Butter

2 cups unbleached all-purpose flour

2 cups sugar

2 teaspoons baking soda

1 tablespoon ground cinnamon

1 teaspoon salt

5 eggs

½ cup vegetable oil

3 cups grated carrots

1 cup chopped nuts of your choice

Serves 10

Growing up, we had dessert only on special occasions, but for some reason my kids have come to expect something sweet every night. As Erma Bombeck said, "Seize the moment. Remember all those women on the *Titanic* who waved off the dessert cart."

. . . .

HOW TO MAKE

1 Preheat the oven to 325°F. Butter and flour a 9- by 13-inch baking dish.

2 Mix the flour, sugar, baking soda, cinnamon, and salt in a large bowl. Beat the eggs and oil in a small bowl and add to the dry mixture, stirring to incorporate. Add the carrots and nuts and mix well.

3 Pour the batter into the pan and bake for 40 to 50 minutes, or until a toothpick inserted in the center comes out clean.

RUM RICE PUDDING

INGREDIENTS

½ cup raisins

¼ cup Mount Gay or other golden rum

½ cup uncooked white rice

½ cup sugar

4 eggs

2¾ cups milk

1 cup unsweetened coconut milk

½ cup unsweetened shredded coconut

Freshly grated nutmeg

Serves 6

One night, while making this dessert, I discovered halfway through the recipe that I was one egg short. I sent Trainer out to the coop in the hope that the girls would cooperate. He took a long time, then came back into the house, running, breathless, excited. He'd seen a snowy owl not 10 feet away. Another reason to have chickens.

. . . .

HOW TO MAKE

1 Soak the raisins in the rum in a small bowl for at least 30 minutes, up to several hours. Cook the rice according to the package directions, then set aside to cool.

2 Preheat the oven to 350°F.

3 Whisk the sugar and eggs together in a 2-quart baking dish. Mix the milk and the coconut milk in a small saucepan over low heat. Toast the coconut in a single layer on a baking sheet in the oven, stirring frequently, until golden, about 10 minutes.

4 Add the milk mixture slowly to the egg and sugar mixture in the baking dish, stirring well. Add the rice, raisins, rum, and toasted coconut, stirring to combine. Generously dust the top with the nutmeg.

5 Place the dish in a large ovenproof roasting pan and add 1 inch of water to the pan. Bake the pudding in this water bath for 1 hour. Test for doneness by inserting a knife in the center; the custard should be set and the residue on the knife moist. Serve warm, or cool on a wire rack and refrigerate to serve cold.

POUND CAKE

INGREDIENTS

1 cup (2 sticks) unsalted butter, softened

½ cup vegetable shortening

3 cups sugar

5 eggs

3 cups unbleached all-purpose flour

1 teaspoon baking powder

½ teaspoon salt

1 cup milk

2 teaspoons vanilla extract

Makes 1 cake

Dating back to the eighteenth century, a pound cake is traditionally made with 1 pound each of flour, butter, eggs, and sugar. I love the simplicity; it reminds me of an old rum-punch ditty from the Grenadines calling for one of sour, two of sweet, three of strong, four of weak.

This makes a large tube cake. If you prefer to halve the recipe, bake the cake in a standard-size loaf pan for 1 hour, or until a knife inserted in the center comes out clean.

● ●

HOW TO MAKE

1 Preheat the oven to 350°F. Grease and flour a 10-inch tube pan.

2 Cream the butter and shortening using an electric mixer, then add the sugar a bit at a time, blending after each addition. Add the eggs one at a time, beating after each addition. Stir together the flour, baking powder, and salt in a bowl and add to the mixer alternately with the milk, starting and ending with the flour. Stir in the vanilla.

3 Pour the batter into the prepared tube pan and bake for 1 hour 30 minutes to 1 hour 45 minutes, or until a knife inserted in the cake comes out clean. Let cool on a wire rack, then invert the pan to remove the cake.

LEMON ICING FOR WHITE CAKE

INGREDIENTS

4 egg yolks

Juice of 2 lemons, plus a little zest

1 cup (2 sticks) butter, softened

2 cups confectioners' sugar

Makes enough to decorate a 9- by 13-inch sheet cake

You'll get more juice out of your lemons if you roll them on the counter before squeezing, or heat them in the microwave for 30 seconds.

● ●

HOW TO MAKE

Mix the egg yolks, lemon juice, and zest using an electric mixer. Beat in the butter, then add the sugar and blend thoroughly. Use immediately, or store in the refrigerator for a few days.

ANGEL FOOD CAKE

INGREDIENTS

1¼ cups confectioners' sugar

1 cup unbleached all-purpose flour

12 egg whites, at room temperature

2 teaspoons vanilla extract

1½ teaspoons cream of tartar

¼ teaspoon salt

1 cup granulated sugar

Raspberry Sauce (recipe follows)

Makes 1 cake

This recipe uses a lot of egg whites. You can freeze the yolks (I recommend marking the quantity, such as "5 EGG YOLKS"). If you are thinking of freezing them for a sweet recipe, add 1 tablespoon of sugar per cup of egg yolk so they don't get lumpy. If you are keeping the yolks for a savory dish, add ½ teaspoon of salt per cup of egg yolk. Thaw in the refrigerator for 8 or so hours before using, and use only in a baked dish.

• •

HOW TO MAKE

1 Preheat the oven to 350°F.

2 Sift together the confectioners' sugar and flour, then set aside.

3 Place the egg whites in a large mixing bowl and add the vanilla, cream of tartar, and salt. Beat on high speed using an electric mixer, gradually adding the granulated sugar. Beat until the sugar is dissolved and stiff peaks form.

4 Gradually add the flour mixture to the egg mixture ½ cup at a time, folding in gently by hand. Spoon the batter into an ungreased 10-inch tube pan. Bake for 40 to 45 minutes, or until a tester inserted in the cake comes out clean. Invert the pan onto the neck of an empty wine bottle and let cool completely before removing the cake. This is delicious served with Raspberry Sauce.

RASPBERRY SAUCE

INGREDIENTS

2 (12-ounce) bags frozen
   raspberries, thawed

¼ cup sugar

1 teaspoon lemon juice

Makes 1¾ cups

This is a beautiful sauce to drizzle over angel food cake, cheesecake, ice cream, even grilled chicken. If I drizzled it over chicken, I might even mince half a jalapeño and add it to the sauce.

• •

HOW TO MAKE

Place the berries in a sieve set on top of a bowl. Using a wooden spoon, press out the juice and pulp and discard the seeds. Add the sugar and lemon juice to the raspberry pulp, stirring to combine. This sauce will keep in the refrigerator for a few days.

EGG WASH

An elixir for pastry, an egg wash will not only make a pie shell golden, but it will also seal edges, patch holes, add a gloss, and generally spruce up your baking. It's made by combining 1 beaten egg with 1 tablespoon of water, milk, half-and-half, or cream.

DESSERTS

A Coop to Be Cooped Up In

Coop choices abound. Some people use a portable Eglu (a hard plastic coop that comes in different colors, made by Omlet), which they move around the yard weekly. Paul Driscoe, a Buddhist architect in Northern California, designed a coop that looks like a mini train car on a track running the length of his garden. With the floor of the coop screened, he moves the coop on the rails every few days, composting his garden as the girls do their business.

I once visited a friend on Martha's Vineyard who had rented chickens for the month of August: a truck pulled up with a little coop on a trailer and left it in her backyard by the sea. She moved it around to compost, and her grandchildren had the pleasure of collecting fresh eggs on vacation. If you want a stationary coop (just beware of the $40 egg), you could create a regal Palais des Poulets, as Martha Stewart did at Turkey Hill.

Despite the fact that the fenced-in yard looks like an Oklahoma duststorm in August, I like our little coop. There's a small window ledge that serves as an additional perch for the girls, from which they eye us in the morning if we take too long to open their door. I hang a wreath and lights on the coop window at Christmas. We have learned over the years that it is safer to give the hens a "run" (a secure, fenced-in outdoor area that is safe from predators by land or by air) than to let them roam free. They need shade in the summer, too, and we have a big old pine tree whose boughs arch protectively over the coop.

ORANGE-WALNUT CAKE

This is a moist, versatile cake. Enclosed in plastic wrap and tied with a ribbon, it's a hostess gift; set out on the counter, it can be served with coffee in the morning or tea in the afternoon. This is a takeoff on a walnut Passover cake, traditionally made without flour for that holiday.

. . . .

INGREDIENTS

2½ cups walnuts

1 tablespoon baking powder

¼ teaspoon salt

⅛ teaspoon freshly grated nutmeg

4 eggs

1 cup lightly packed brown sugar

½ cup orange juice

1 tablespoon finely grated orange zest

1 teaspoon vanilla extract

½ cup extra-virgin olive oil

Confectioners' sugar

Serves 8

HOW TO MAKE

1 Preheat the oven to 350°F. Spray a 9-inch springform pan with nonstick cooking spray.

2 Finely grind the walnuts in a food processor. Combine the walnuts with the baking powder, salt, and nutmeg in a medium bowl.

3 Beat the eggs lightly in a large bowl, then add the brown sugar, orange juice, orange zest, vanilla, and olive oil, mixing well. Add the walnut mixture to the egg mixture, beating just until blended. Transfer the batter to the prepared pan and place on a rimmed baking sheet.

4 Bake for about 1 hour, until a tester inserted in the center comes out clean. Cool completely in the pan on a wire rack. Remove the ring and dust the cake with confectioners' sugar before serving.

CHOCOLATE ANGEL PIE

This is a cool, light dessert from Verna Thompson that will satisfy any chocoholic.

. . . .

INGREDIENTS

Butter

2 egg whites

⅛ teaspoon salt

⅛ teaspoon cream of tartar

½ cup granulated sugar

½ cup finely chopped walnuts or pecans

1½ teaspoons dark Jamaican rum

4 ounces semisweet chocolate

3 tablespoons strong hot brewed coffee

2 cups heavy cream

Pinch of confectioners' sugar

Fresh mint leaves

Fresh raspberries

Makes one 8-inch pie

HOW TO MAKE

1 Preheat the oven to 300°F and lightly butter an 8-inch pie plate.

2 Beat the egg whites with a rotary beater or a whisk until foamy. Add the salt and the cream of tartar. Continue beating until the mixture forms soft peaks. Add the granulated sugar gradually and continue beating until the mixture is very stiff. Fold in the nuts and ½ teaspoon of the rum.

3 Turn the mixture into the prepared pie plate. Make a nestlike shell, building the sides of the mixture up ½ inch above the edge of the pie plate. Bake for 50 to 55 minutes. Let the shell cool completely.

4 Put the chocolate in the top of a double boiler over medium heat. When melted, add the hot coffee and blend. Remove from the heat and let cool until thickened. Then add the remaining 1 teaspoon of rum to the mixture. Whip 1 cup of the cream until soft peaks form and fold the whipped cream into the chocolate mixture. Turn the filling into the meringue shell and chill at for least 2 hours.

5 To serve, whip the remaining 1 cup of cream. Add a sprinkling of Jamaican rum, if you want (much as you'd add vanilla), and a bit of confectioners' sugar. Place a dollop of the whipped cream on each slice of pie and garnish with the mint leaves and raspberries.

PECAN PIE

Pecan pie is a staple of many holiday meals. Having grown up fewer than 20 miles from Plymouth Rock, I serve it every year at Thanksgiving, along with apple pie and often pumpkin pie, even though the Pilgrims never had pies; there were no ovens in Plymouth, and by the time the settlers arrived on Cape Cod, they'd used up most, if not all, of their sugar. Pecan pie is a French dish, created by seventeenth-century settlers in New Orleans who were introduced to pecans by Native Americans.

INGREDIENTS

- 4 eggs
- ¾ cup sugar
- Pinch of salt
- 1 cup chopped or whole pecans
- 1½ cups dark corn syrup
- 4 tablespoons butter, melted
- 1 teaspoon vanilla extract
- 1 (9-inch) pie shell

Serves 6

HOW TO MAKE

1 Preheat the oven to 450°F. Arrange the shell in a pie plate.

2 Beat the eggs in a large bowl, then add the sugar, salt, pecans, corn syrup, melted butter, and vanilla and blend well. Pour the filling into the pie shell. Bake for 10 minutes, then reduce the temperature to 320°F and bake for 45 minutes longer, until the filling is set. Let cool on a wire rack before serving.

MERINGUE COOKIES

INGREDIENTS

2 egg whites

1 teaspoon vanilla extract

⅛ teaspoon cream of tartar

⅛ teaspoon salt

¾ cup sugar

¾ cup chocolate chips

½ cup pecans, chopped

Makes 30 cookies

I found this recipe in my great-grandmother's recipe box. Both she and my great-grandfather were from Boston but met in the Isthmus of Panama. He was returning to Boston from California, having spent a few months on a farm on the West Coast recovering from a train accident he'd been in near the Hoosac Tunnel, close to where I now live. She and her mother were traveling to California from Boston. When she returned, he courted her and they married and eventually raised seven children.

HOW TO MAKE

1 Preheat the oven to 300°F. Line a baking sheet with parchment paper.

2 Beat the egg whites in a medium bowl with the vanilla, cream of tartar, and salt until soft peaks form. Add the sugar gradually, beating until stiff, glossy peaks form. Fold in the chocolate chips and the nuts.

3 Drop the dough by rounded teaspoonsful onto the prepared baking sheet, spacing them about 2 inches apart. Bake for 25 minutes. Let cool on a wire rack.

⬤ LEFTOVER EGG WHITES

You can freeze egg whites. Just drop them into an ice-cube tray (1 egg white per compartment) and stick in the freezer. Once frozen, transfer to a ziplock freezer bag. To use, thaw in the refrigerator. For any recipe calling for whipped egg whites, be sure to bring them to room temperature before beating.

VANILLA ICE CREAM

INGREDIENTS

4 eggs

1 cup sugar

2 cups heavy cream

2 cups half-and-half

1 tablespoon vanilla extract

Whole milk (to fill 1-gallon freezer)

Makes 1 gallon

For me, homemade vanilla ice cream conjures up memories of sitting on the porch on a summer night, with fireflies, music, and sparklers. My friend Liddy Doherty's family always made it on the Fourth of July, after the parade and fireworks, for their friends and neighbors. Joe will crank up the ice-cream freezer and make it for a crowd, and also just for us, for no particular occasion — it's that easy. You can halve this recipe for a small gathering. You don't cook the eggs, so be sure your eggs are from a safe source.

• •

HOW TO MAKE

1 Beat the eggs in a large bowl until creamy and light. Add the sugar, cream, half-and-half, and vanilla. Cover and refrigerate until cold, at least 3 hours.

2 Pour into a 1-gallon ice-cream freezer container. Finish filling with milk to within a few inches of the top. Freeze according to the manufacturer's instructions.

OREO ICE CREAM

Despite efforts to bake my own cookies, my kids love Oreos. They'll dip them in milk until they're mushy, then eat them with a spoon. In this recipe, eggs from your own hens are best, as the eggs are not cooked.

. . . .

INGREDIENTS

4 eggs

2 cups sugar

4 cups heavy cream

3 tablespoons vanilla extract

3 cups crushed Oreo cookies

Whole milk (to fill 1-gallon freezer)

Makes 1 gallon

HOW TO MAKE

1 Beat the eggs in a large bowl until creamy and light. Add the sugar and beat until thick. Add the cream and vanilla and mix well. Cover and refrigerate for at least 3 hours.

2 Pour into a 1-gallon ice-cream freezer container. Add the cookie pieces, then fill to the top with milk and freeze according to the manufacturer's instructions.

"In the broken nest there are no whole eggs."

— Chinese proverb

ESPRESSO ICE CREAM

INGREDIENTS

4 eggs

2 cups heavy cream

½ cup ground espresso beans

2 cups half-and-half

1 cup sugar

1 tablespoon vanilla extract

½ teaspoon salt

Whole milk (to fill 1-gallon freezer)

Serves 4

This is more of an adult ice cream, with its rich, intense flavor. You could substitute other coffee beans for the espresso beans. Use only eggs from a safe source, as they will not be cooked.

HOW TO MAKE

1 Beat the eggs in a large bowl until creamy and light. Warm the cream in a small saucepan, add the ground espresso beans, and then turn off the heat and let the mixture steep for 10 to 15 minutes.

2 Strain through a fine-mesh sieve and let cool. Add to the egg mixture, along with the half-and-half, sugar, vanilla, and salt. Cover and refrigerate until cold, at least 3 hours.

3 Pour into a 1-gallon ice-cream freezer container. Finish filling with milk to within a few inches of the top. Freeze according to the manufacturer's instructions.

LEMON SHERBET

With its light, tangy taste and strong lemony flavor, this is a refreshing dessert for spring or summer. Beaten egg whites are incorporated into the sherbet to give it a light texture. You'll get more volume if you bring the egg whites to room temperature before whipping them. You can easily bump up the recipe to serve a crowd, or to freeze and serve later. Make sure your eggs are from a safe source, as they are not cooked.

INGREDIENTS

⅔ cup sugar

½ cup fresh lemon juice (2–3 lemons)

1 cup half-and-half or light cream

1 cup whole milk

2 egg whites

¼ teaspoon salt

Zest of 1 lemon, chopped very fine

Makes 1½ quarts

HOW TO MAKE

1 Stir the sugar and lemon juice together in a medium bowl until the sugar is almost dissolved. Add the half-and-half and milk to the lemon-sugar mixture, beating with a whisk to combine. Put the mixture in the refrigerator to chill while you prepare the egg whites.

2 Put the egg whites in a small bowl, add the salt, and beat until stiff. Fold the egg whites into the lemon mixture with a slotted spoon. Add the zest and blend gently. Transfer to an ice-cream freezer container and freeze according to the manufacturer's instructions.

LEMON MOUSSE

Don't be alarmed by the white strands you find inside an egg after you crack it open. They're protein, and edible. The fresher the egg, the more prominent the chalazae ("hailstones" in Greek), which serve as shock absorbers for the yolk, keeping it unbroken.

INGREDIENTS

4 egg yolks

1 cup sugar

½ cup fresh lemon juice (2–3 lemons)

1 tablespoon grated lemon zest

½ teaspoon salt

1 tablespoon powdered gelatin, softened in ¼ cup cold water

4 egg whites

Serves 4–6

HOW TO MAKE

1 Beat the egg yolks in the top of a double boiler, then add ½ cup of the sugar, the lemon juice, the zest, and the salt. Cook over low heat until the mixture thickens slightly and coats the back of a wooden spoon. Add the gelatin and water and stir until dissolved. Remove from the heat and let cool.

2 When beginning to set, beat the egg whites with the remaining ½ cup of sugar until stiff peaks form, then fold into the lemon mixture. Chill until set, for at least 1 hour or overnight.

LEMON SQUARES

INGREDIENTS

For the Crust

- 1 cup (2 sticks) butter, softened
- 2 cups unbleached all-purpose flour
- ½ cup confectioners' sugar
- ½ teaspoon salt

For the Filling

- 4 eggs
- 2 cups granulated sugar
- 6 tablespoons unbleached all-purpose flour
- 6 tablespoons lemon juice
- 1 tablespoon grated lemon zest
- ½ teaspoon vanilla extract
- Confectioners' sugar

Makes 15 squares

Lemon squares remind me of boats, perhaps because I was introduced to the tart treats by Liz Wheeler on my first boat delivery. After I graduated from Tufts University, I was waitressing in Bar Harbor, Maine, living with my cousin Doug, when we were offered the job of crewing on a 40-foot Bermuda Hinckley that needed delivering from Mount Desert Island to Virgin Gorda. If you don't know boats, that's like someone paying you to drive a Maserati from Paris to the Riviera. I leapt at the chance but didn't realize at the time how smart the captain was to assemble a crew of four that consisted of him, my cousin and me, and Liz as cook. No Dinty Moore stew out of a can for us; Liz was a maestro who could whip up extraordinary meals in wretched conditions. Liz and I went on to write *The Yachting Cookbook* together, and this is adapted from one of her recipes.

HOW TO MAKE

1 Preheat the oven to 350°F. Butter a 9- by 13-inch baking dish.

2 For the crust, mix the butter, flour, confectioners' sugar, and salt in a bowl, then pat into the prepared baking dish. Bake for 15 minutes, or until golden.

3 For the filling, beat the eggs in a large bowl and mix in the granulated sugar, flour, lemon juice, lemon zest, and vanilla. Beat until fluffy. Pour over the baked crust and return to the oven for 30 minutes, or until filling is set. Transfer to a wire rack to cool, then dust with confectioners' sugar and cut into squares.

LEMON MERINGUE PIE

INGREDIENTS

For the Crust

Pastry for a single-crust 9-inch pie

For the Filling

1 cup sugar

5 tablespoons cornstarch

Pinch of salt

1½ cups hot water

4 egg yolks (reserve the whites for the meringue)

Juice of 2 lemons

1 teaspoon lemon zest

1 tablespoon unsalted butter

For the Meringue

4 egg whites

Pinch of cream of tartar

3 tablespoons sugar

Makes one 9-inch pie

Isabel and I make this pie for Trainer when we have too many eggs, as it's a favorite of his. Isabel loves to cook, and she's pretty good at separating the eggs. If you've lost one too many yolks into the white abyss, crack each egg gently over a strainer, and the white will flow through it while the yolk catches in the web.

HOW TO MAKE

1 Preheat the oven to 450ºF.

2 Line a 9-inch pie plate with the dough and prick in several places. Place foil over the dough and place weights on top. Bake for 12 minutes. Remove from the oven, remove the weights and foil, lower the oven temperature to 350ºF, and bake for 10 minutes, or until the crust is golden brown. Cool on a wire rack. Leave the oven on.

3 For the filling, combine the sugar, cornstarch, and salt in a medium saucepan. Gradually add the hot water, and bring to a boil over medium heat, stirring constantly, until the mixture is thick, bubbly, and whitish, about 5 minutes. Remove from the heat.

4 Beat the yolks in a small bowl, then add ½ cup of the cornstarch mixture, whisking to blend. Pour the mixture back into the saucepan, stir, and return to medium heat. Add the lemon juice and zest and cook for 5 minutes, stirring constantly. Add the butter near the end. Remove from the heat and pour into the pie shell.

5 For the meringue, beat the egg whites with the cream of tartar in a medium bowl until they are foamy and hold soft peaks. Keep beating, adding the sugar gradually, until the whites are shiny and the peaks are stiff. Lavish the meringue over the filling. Return to the oven and bake 10 to 15 minutes, until the meringue is golden. It's helpful to let the pie sit for an hour before serving, though it's not necessary.

"There are two kinds of fears: rational and irrational — or, in simpler terms, fears that make sense and fears that don't. For instance, the Baudelaire orphans have a fear of Count Olaf, which makes perfect sense, because he is an evil man who wants to destroy them. But if they were afraid of lemon meringue pie, this would be an irrational fear, because lemon meringue pie is delicious and would never hurt a soul."

— Lemony Snicket, *A Series of Unfortunate Events*

METRIC CONVERSIONS

Unless you have finely calibrated measuring equipment, conversions between U.S. and metric measurements will be somewhat inexact. It's important to convert the measurements for all of the ingredients in a recipe to maintain the same proportions as the original.

GENERAL FORMULA FOR METRIC CONVERSION

Ounces to grams	multiply ounces by 28.35
Grams to ounces	multiply grams by 0.035
Pounds to grams	multiply pounds by 453.5
Pounds to kilograms	multiply pounds by 0.45
Cups to liters	multiply cups by 0.24
Fahrenheit to Celsius	subtract 32 from Fahrenheit temperature, multiply by 5, then divide by 9
Celsius to Fahrenheit	multiply Celsius temperature by 9, divide by 5, then add 32

APPROXIMATE EQUIVALENTS BY VOLUME

U.S.	Metric
1 teaspoon	5 milliliters
1 tablespoon	15 milliliters
¼ cup	60 milliliters
½ cup	120 milliliters
1 cup	230 milliliters
1¼ cups	300 milliliters
1½ cups	360 milliliters
2 cups	460 milliliters
2½ cups	600 milliliters
3 cups	700 milliliters
4 cups (1 quart)	0.95 liter
1.06 quarts	1 liter
4 quarts (1 gallon)	3.8 liters

APPROXIMATE EQUIVALENTS BY WEIGHT

U.S.	Metric
¼ ounce	7 grams
½ ounce	14 grams
1 ounce	28 grams
1¼ ounces	35 grams
1½ ounces	40 grams
2½ ounces	70 grams
4 ounces	112 grams
5 ounces	140 grams
8 ounces	228 grams
10 ounces	280 grams
15 ounces	425 grams
16 ounces (1 pound)	454 grams
0.035 ounce	1 gram
1.75 ounces	50 grams
3.5 ounces	100 grams
8.75 ounces	250 grams
1.1 pounds	500 grams
2.2 pounds	1 kilogram

INDEX

Page numbers in *italics* indicate photographs.

CRACK INTO FRESH FLAVORS
WITH MORE BOOKS FROM STOREY

by Olwen Woodier

Apple pie is just the beginning! Discover the versatility of this iconic fruit with 125 delicious recipes for any meal, including apple frittata, pork chops with apple cream sauce, apple pizza, apple butter, and more.

by Andrea Chesman

Get the most from your home-grown foods with this friendly and comprehensive guide to gathering, preserving, and eating the fruits of your labor. You'll learn how to can fresh produce, mill flour, render lard, make butter and cheese, and much more!

by Rachael Narins

Make your skillet sizzle! These 40 recipes show off the versatility of this affordable and timeless cooking method, from cast-iron classics like cornbread, pan pizza, and the perfect grilled cheese sandwich to future favorites like Korean fried chicken, skillet catfish, and s'mores.

by Lauren K. Stein

Capture the playful side of cooking with charming, full-page illustrations for 75 veggie-centric recipes. From pineapple cilantro salsa and asparagus apple salad to a kale egg scramble, these simple recipes celebrate the unbeatable flavors of fresh ingredients.

by Ken Haedrich

Maple syrup isn't just for breakfast! From pancakes and scones to fondue, salad dressing, grilled salmon, shrimp and sausage kabobs, cheesecake, and much more, discover how the taste of pure maple syrup enhances any meal.

Join the conversation. Share your experience with this book, learn more about Storey Publishing's authors, and read original essays and book excerpts at storey.com. Look for our books wherever quality books are sold or by calling 800-441-5700.